W9-BWT-293

LET **LOVE** HAVE THE LAST WORD

≡ΛHIP 2022
JUN 21–23, LAS VEGAS, NV

Enjoy this book compliments of

zipari

Common

ALSO BY COMMON

One Day It'll All Make Sense

LET LOVE

HAVE THE

LAST WORD

A MEMOIR

COMMON

WITH MENSAH DEMARY

ATRIA PAPERBACK

NEW YORK · LONDON · TORONTO · SYDNEY · NEW DELHI

ATRIA
PAPERBACK

An Imprint of Simon & Schuster, Inc.
1230 Avenue of the Americas
New York, NY 10020

Copyright © 2021 by Think Common Entertainment, Inc.

All rights reserved, including the right to reproduce this book or portions
thereof in any form whatsoever. For information, address Atria Books Subsidiary
Rights Department, 1230 Avenue of the Americas, New York, NY 10020.

This Atria Books paperback edition February 2021

ATRIA PAPERBACK and colophon are trademarks of Simon & Schuster, Inc.

For information about special discounts for bulk purchases, please
contact Simon & Schuster Special Sales at 1-866-506-1949 or
business@simonandschuster.com.

Manufactured in the United States of America

10 9 8 7 6 5 4 3

Library of Congress Cataloging-in-Publication Data is available.

ISBN 978-1-5011-3316-9 (paperback)

FROM THE AUTHOR

Dear Reader,

*No one has it all figured out; I certainly do not.
This memoir is intended to share my process of
digging deeper, making mistakes, trying again,
and continuing to trust God that we all have an
opportunity to live in freedom, love, and positivity
when we do the work on self. Thank you for taking
this journey with me. I hope, through my story, you
also find tools and encouragement to apply love, to
overcome all.*

Love,
Common

PART ONE

" We can no longer afford to worship the god of hate or bow before the altar of retaliation. As Arnold Toynbee says: 'Love is the ultimate force that makes for the saving choice of life and good against the damning choice of death and evil. Therefore, the first hope in our inventory must be the hope that love is going to have the last word.' "

—*Dr. Martin Luther King Jr.*

A man is worked upon by what he works on. He may carve out his circumstances, but his circumstances will carve him out as well.

—**Frederick Douglass**

———

I was standing in front of a full-length mirror, in the middle of a fashion designer's studio in Beverly Hills. It was hot outside, the clear blue sky was hazy, and the sun warmed the concrete. My truck was parked along the curb, and I was thinking about a peaceful, quiet drive. In the meantime, I looked at myself in the mirror.

Kendrick's new album *DAMN.* was on shuffle, and I bobbed my head while my assistant, Aun, sat next to my charging phone, checking her own phone and answering emails, answering texts, cleaning up the calendar, all for the sake of me. I was the center of this work, and—I kept looking at myself.

I knew who I saw when I saw the face staring back at me— it had been more or less the same face for forty-plus years now—yet I thought: *Who* is *that? Is that* me? Someone asked me a question about a jacket, and I shook my head. "Nah," I said.

I could hear Micaela, my stylist, sighing. She was there on the laptop, or I should say *in my laptop*, propped up on a chair; she watched my fitting from her remote location via FaceTime. I asked her where she was at, and she named the city, said she was working and visiting friends, and I told her I had just been out there myself, and I couldn't wait to get back.

I am blessed with this opportunity of mine to move about the world . . . it is vital, and it has only increased as time goes by. From vans and buses, touring around the country, doing campus shows back in the early 1990s, to now, present day, flying across the country and around the world.

At the time of this fitting, I was in Los Angeles, my home away from Chicago, and the fitting was for a benefit concert I'd been asked to do. There was a red-carpet appearance scheduled prior to the show.

"Try this on." I slipped my arms through a dark-brown jacket, this one more my taste. I jerked my shoulders up and down. "Feels a little snug but it looks dope," I said, staring at my reflection again. I turned to the left, then to the right; I checked to see where the jacket ended—at my hips, almost a perfect fit. "I think that one," Micaela said through the laptop, "but we have another one in green. Let's try that one. And let's swap out the shoes for the all-white sneakers."

And like that, the stylist's assistants buzzed around me with swift movements. I stood there in front of the mirror, and asked Aun what time it was. "Just before two," she said, looking up from her phone. She reminded me about the meetings I had later in the day. *Meetings.* I was to sit down with a director who was shooting a film I wanted in on, and I had a call with a cop from a city police department who was helping me prepare for another possible role, a homicide detective.

Then I had scripts to read, and phone calls to return. I wanted to get to the recording studio later, but the possibility seemed more remote by the minute—hence the desire to go for a drive. At least there, in my truck, I could rap to myself over some instrumentals, or to no music at all. Rapping to myself without purpose, only because I loved to do it.

Speaking of love, I've been rapping for more than twenty-five years now. I would rap for free. I would rap if I lived on the streets. I would rap if I was a preacher, a prisoner, or a politician. I was paid $5,000 for my first album, *Can I Borrow a Dollar?*—an amount that was split among three people. The label got us for the cheap, no doubt, but I was grateful at the time to be paid *anything* for something I loved to do and would have done no matter the cost.

That I've since received more money for rapping speaks to perseverance, I suppose, or market forces. Rapping is my release, my art, my way of expression. It's a desire that comes from my spirit, and whenever I can appease the desire to rap, I do. And if I can't do it in a studio, then I'll go for a drive, alone, and do it there, happily and at peace.

The fitting went on for a little while longer. I tried on a couple more outfits, made my choices, which Micaela approved with a thumbs-up from the laptop, and said my goodbyes and thanks to the staff as Aun and I departed. After trying on the fresh clothes, I felt dressed down when I was back in my T-shirt and basketball shorts, my usual outfit when I work out at the gym with my trainer; I often get along with him, but at the time, he and I were having a slight disagreement. It was about politics, something involving the president, barely six months into his first term, who had everyone on edge, it seemed, prepared for disaster. After Barack Obama, the world felt uncertain and unstable, unpredictable, and dark.

When Aun and I stepped outside, the Southern California heat assaulted us. "Damn," I said, shielding my eyes from the sun with my hand. Aun and I were walking down the sidewalk, hardly a few yards from my stylist's building, when someone shouted me out. "Are you Common?"

I didn't even see him until he said my name, a slim white dude wearing shorts and a red shirt; the shirt matched his Nike trainers, and the hatchback he pointed to when he said, "I was just parking my car and I saw you step out and I was like, 'Yo, is that Common?' Your music changed my life, and it blessed my life, too." He told me his name, and I shook his hand. He said he was a yoga teacher, and a personal trainer. "I trained Kobe," he said. I had no idea if that was true or if he was just running a hustle; in either case, he gave me his business card. "I'd love to train with you," he said. I said, "Cool," then thanked him for the card as I climbed into my truck, started the ignition, and peeled out. I started the day staring at myself in the mirror; likewise, this memoir is a reflection of me as I examine myself and consider love from its beautiful dimensions.

Love makes your soul crawl out from its hiding place.

—Zora Neale Hurston

—————

My name is Rashid, and I do not necessarily know more about love than you do. The emotion feels elusive, as well as the knowledge, the understanding—the *meaning*, in other words. Why do I love? Why do I bother? I suppose, in thinking about it, there is something human in the desire to love and to be loved; those things are treated as separate desires, wants, but maybe they are the same coin. It is love, on both sides— you and I, he and she, they and them—that adds dimensions to the emotion. It reflects from all angles the various temperatures and viewpoints of love, and no matter how one might feel in the moment, and this I can relate to personally, there is no one true story.

In the midst of a new breakup, or some years after a past one, there is, I think, a habit to reconsider all that happened between two people, to see if your role in it was as bad as you really perceive it, in the hopes of perhaps forgiving yourself. This doesn't mean you necessarily did anything wrong or hurtful to the other person. On the contrary, sometimes relationships simply end, without blame, without guilty parties. Or maybe I'm wrong. Maybe, in the end, there is always someone who is at fault. Is that me? Was that the case when such-and-such relationship with so-and-so deteriorated after so many hopes, visions, fantasies, of a shared life?

If it was me, if I am in fact guilty, then I have to ask myself the questions, here and now, from that single point in my mind, that one rotating planet in space, my world. Here, I am now in my midforties, and I am experiencing, comparatively speaking, a more successful life than before.

To be recognized for my art, to have been in the game, so to speak, for so many years now, to be able to produce, then give back to the community, all of this, to say nothing of wealth, has been—to keep it real—all I've ever wanted. Then again, it is never really *all*, is it? The more we attain, the more we wish for, as if we're scratching off tasks from a to-do list. For me, becoming a husband, one half of a long-term and committed intimate relationship, remains unfinished, though I've gotten close a few times. *We* did.

I could list each of their names now, but there's no need to get into specifics. In love, each person has their own story to tell, and it's not my place to speak for other people. But—I was in love. If love is truly eternal, then maybe I still am, after so many moments since the end of our time together. But this isn't all about broken hearts and sad songs; this is quiet reflection in the middle of the night, in bed, alone, thinking, just thinking, about everything and nothing.

I'm not interested in presenting prescriptive ideas that prop up a gender's point of view at the expense of dismissing another. Rather, I take the position that I know nothing about love, and neither do you; at the same time, I know everything about love, as do you. I have my experiences, and you have yours; there are small, human truths within the universal truth, the one truth. This I call God, the Most High, and from here I try to move through the world with Him and His universal truth in mind, as practiced by Christ and the prophets, the leaders, the women and men who between life and death tried to live for someone other than themselves, an act of true love.

It feels as if no one wants to be a hero anymore, nor do people seek them out. The sentiment is a little played out now, maybe; in the quest for individual success and truth, to make it known where they stand on this or that issue, provided they say anything at all about a thing, I don't know if it matters to people whether or not they're viewed as heroes. It matters to me.

I have a few heroes in my life, those who've inspired me. Dr. Martin Luther King Jr. is one hero, as well as Muhammad Ali, and Dr. Maya Angelou—these are just the first names that come to mind. Each one lived an authentic life, which I think is invaluable and necessary if one is wanting to live with love, live in love, and find and maintain a love for oneself, and to love others.

King, Ali, and Angelou loved other people, loved the Black community, and found their own individual ways to serve the community, but I think it all starts with love of self. That's not to say God is placed second on the list, if there is such a list, of who should be loved in one's life.

God is love, sang Marvin Gaye, but to serve God and to serve other people, families, and communities, you have to care for yourself; you have to love yourself. And as clichéd as this sounds, because I think we all know and speak on the need to love ourselves, the practice of loving yourself is difficult to establish, and there's no one way to do it.

To me, heroes appear as though they move with a singular focus and a laser-sharp dedication with a goal or a new world in mind, something that is not easily attainable but is possible so long as you resolve to pursue it. All of my heroes loved themselves differently and they each found their path in life.

And I've become more familiar with the lives of my heroes. I had my ideas in mind, for example, of how Dr. King was as a man of the people and of the pulpit. But since my work on the film *Selma*, I have a greater appreciation for him even though the movie showed that Dr. King had flaws—which was vital for us to see: A man routinely mythologized for his work and his deeds was still a human, imperfect and hurtful to those who loved him the most, engaged in a constant back-and-forth recalibration of his life to achieve and manifest his greatest dreams and hopes, all while sometimes failing to maintain that balance. I can relate.

I'm proud of the work I've done throughout my career, and I give back whenever I can, in time, in money, and in effort, and yet my daughter, Omoye, questioned my love for her, questioned whether or not I fight to be present in her life, make the effort to *be there* as often as I can, and more so, in her world. I've felt guilty at times. I love my daughter, but in the pursuit of a career, greatness, in part to provide for her and my family in general, I've hurt her with my lack of presence, my lack of fight.

I don't know if I am Omoye's hero, or one of them, but I know I always wanted to be one for her; a part of being a hero means having to carry the weight, and to get back up when you fall. Acknowledge who you are, then with resolution pursue your higher self, that ideal and perfect version of yourself, reflecting God's light, knowing that you will fail over and over again, but you pursue anyway. You live your life the best way you can, but the important thing is to live, and to do it with love.

I don't want to be worshipped like a hero; no one has to point at me and say, *That's a hero right there.* But I do look toward other people I identify as heroes; maybe *role model* is a more appropriate label for them, because I understand that while I must do all that I can, on my own terms, to get from point A to B in this world, there are those people who've done it before me, who did it better, who are still doing it. What I said about love applies to anything, everything: I know nothing, and everything.

Work is love made visible.

—*Kahlil Gibran,* **The Prophet**

———

My mother and late father gave me the name Rashid, but I named myself Common—well, Common Sense, but that's a whole other story—back in 1992, and created a persona, a division, a separation between Rashid and the entertainer (although Common is authentically Rashid). Common was born from a love of hip-hop, an art form that paved for me a path toward a freedom I had dreamed about since I was a little boy in South Side Chicago. There, I watched Michael Jackson moonwalk across the television screen, and as a ball boy for the Chicago Bulls, I saw firsthand how Michael Jordan soared to the rim; later, I started to rap, and listened closely to Rakim and Big Daddy Kane, wanting to be a dope emcee like them.

I wanted to impress my friends with my music, my boys from Chicago who loved hip-hop as much as me, who saw in the genre a value that, ironically enough, could hardly be put into words. Hip-hop was the space where I could unleash my voice, speak my truth in a way that felt fresh and relevant. I loved hip-hop; I knew it from the beginning. I haven't stopped moving to the music since, even as the sounds have changed, as have the new emcees, and me. I'm an actor now. I am also a philanthropist, a public speaker, an activist; I produce television shows; am a spokesperson for brands; and I'm still a son, a father, a friend, a man of God. But not a husband.

It's human nature to feel the absence of things, the lack, more than the bounties, the presence of people and blessings, the very present itself. I wake up early each morning around five or six, and the first thing I do is meditate. Maybe it is more like silent prayer, because in these moments I feel especially close to God, and sometimes I might pray for clarity in regard to a problem—an issue with Omoye, or something selfish, like wanting an opportunity to play a role I desire after reading some script—as the sun rises over the hills in Los Angeles.

Sitting quietly, I try to enter a certain space, something like the creative flow of freestyling, where I come up with a verse on the spot, in the moment. Freestyling is to rap in the present; similarly, my meditative space brings me back to the present where God and love exist. Love is a verb, I've heard throughout the years, not a noun; to love someone is to take action, to *do* something in love's name. Love counts most in the present moment.

Each of our actions has its own past, and its own future, and we have the ability to reflect both backward and forward in time. Not that we always remember the past as a moment that really happened, and no one can predict the future, but in our everyday experience, this is how our minds and hearts work. Over and over, we move forward in hopes of a brighter, oncoming day, all while carrying shame about a thing that happened yesterday or twenty years ago.

Nevertheless, in love, the present matters. There is always an opportunity to learn and experience something new, to expose ourselves to wisdom by recognizing the humanity in others, to see through their eyes our one world; in this way, with love, we enter an empathetic space, as if it were a portal to a whole new world.

Love provides an opportunity for us to connect on a higher plane, to our higher selves. I truly believe there is, in each of us, a true version of ourselves. I try to attain this higher version of myself through prayer and meditation; through spirituality and the belief in us, in myself; I try to get out of my own way. I try to push aside my ego to learn something about the world, about my life, something real, and true, something sincere and beyond the surface.

There's so much pain and suffering; instead of one World War, we have multiple wars happening all around the world. People walk thousands of miles over treacherous terrain, many with children, in flight from burning homes and neighborhoods hollowed out by bombs. Women can't walk the streets or do their jobs without harassment and assault by men; Black men and women rot in American prisons; and our government leaders are ineffective, or don't care, or have their own agendas, treating their own citizens as the enemies in the name of retaining electability among their bases.

Divisions everywhere, a human species splintered into sects, sides, and demographics. It's too much; I don't know what to do about any of this—but I want to *do* something, now, in the present. And in the present there is love, which is conscious and compassionate activity toward the betterment and care for yourself and others, even if it's just one person, even if it's a stranger, a homeless man asking for a dollar, a traveler who needs directions to a destination.

But I can't lie. I feel foolish for offering love as a weapon; there is, I admit, doubt in my heart about love's effectiveness among so much horror, so much suffering. I do believe in the life of Jesus, the man. You don't have to be a Christian to recognize Jesus as a revolutionary, as a man who, armed with love and faith, stood in opposition to power that eventually seized, whipped, and crucified him for awakening minds to their capabilities as people.

To love God, no matter the name, and no matter the religion, is to make a wholehearted reach toward the universal, to come to see for oneself that in spite of the lonely feelings we have as individual people, each of us can still stand on our own two feet, supported by a higher, deeper power.

All work is empty save when there is love; And when you work with love you bind yourself to yourself, and to one another, and to God.

—*Kahlil Gibran*, **The Prophet**

———

I t was late, or early, that weird hour before dawn, maybe four in the morning. I was at home in Los Angeles. I couldn't sleep. I was preparing for my role in a movie that was beginning to shoot, and I had to get up and use the bathroom, so I was already awake when my phone vibrated. I could see on the screen that it was Omoye. There's nothing more terrifying than getting a call at that hour from your child or any loved one.

Omoye, twenty years old at the time, a sophomore at Howard University, had never called me at four in the morning. *Is she okay? Does she need my help? Is she safe?* All of these thoughts, and more, repeated rapidly in my head, over and over again, in the same amount of time, just a few seconds, that it took me to pick up the phone and answer.

Her speech was slow and slurred, but I understood everything she said. Omoye had been drinking, it seemed, and I wanted to make sure she was somewhere safe, that she was not in danger. I asked her if she was okay, and she replied yes. It's always weird to hear your child when they're a little drunk, but I had been drinking at her age, too, and I couldn't hold it against her for getting a little bubbly. I wasn't stressed about it. I just wanted to know she was safe.

My heart was still racing a bit, but everything seemed to be fine. I thought for a moment how great it was that our relationship had grown to a place that she knew she could, and actually wanted to, call me anytime. Even if she was bubbly and just wanted to hear my voice.

I wanted to hug her. It's hard not being around your child when you want to reach out and touch them the most, just to put hands on your child with a touch to confirm their safety and reaffirm your love for them. It's not a question of being an overprotective parent who hovers. But I am a good father, or at least that's what I thought as our phone conversation ended.

About three minutes later, my phone vibrated again. This time it was a notification, a text message from Omoye. And moments later my phone vibrated again. It was Omoye calling. I immediately realized there had been more to the first call than just touching down with her dad.

Omoye was upset with me. At first, it was because of my reaction to her phone call earlier. I had seemed too laid-back to her, or perhaps I hadn't sounded as concerned as I had really felt. I apologized to her, and tried to choose the right words, better words, so she could understand that I really was worried about her. But of course, the thing with alcohol is that it lowers your inhibitions. So while Omoye was upset that I hadn't been concerned *in the moment*, in reality she began to unpack her feelings about me as a father, from the perspective of a daughter who had lived and experienced it every day for twenty years, including all my absences.

It sounds like a cliché, I know, but my life has changed since becoming a father. Many of the selfish and self-centered habits and thoughts, all of the ways in which I wanted to put myself first, had to give way and make space for someone else's needs. And in doing these simple yet very important things, we make our children the center of our lives. They need us, their parents and guardians, to love them so they can survive, literally.

Things get a little more complicated as time passes, however, as our children grow older. You begin to see life from their point of view. I know every relationship is different, but at least with Omoye I've tried to foster a positive environment where she can come and talk to me at any time, for any reason, and I'll be there for her. But that wasn't always the case. How could it be? She needed me, and I needed to provide for her and her mother, and for myself, so I spent my time out in the world, touring, traveling, meeting, and performing.

It wasn't easy, and things didn't happen for me overnight. I had to grind, to hustle, just as my mother taught me, to work hard, to apply myself, and to challenge myself in whatever endeavor I pursued, no matter the results. And yet, I thought of myself as a "good father," which is to say I had these ideas in my mind of what a "bad father" looked like, of how he conducted himself. I could do better, be better, for a little girl I loved more than any other person on Earth. But my little girl was a young Black woman arriving at her own conclusions about how things went down in her life. She had her own point of view, one that she decided to share with me that night.

Though our kids need clothes and want new toys, these aren't the things they ask of us, when you really think about it. Granted, Omoye might've asked for a couple of dollars to hold to go to the movies with her friends, but that was a want, a desire, not a need. But for me, the status or dollars don't mean as much if I am out of balance, if the people in my life feel they have to question whether or not I care about them.

This was at the heart of my late-night conversation with Omoye. She didn't know if I cared about her, and that night wasn't the first time she had felt that way. That hit me hard. She felt as though I didn't fight for her during her childhood when, as I've said, I spent a lot of that time on the road. I tried to listen and reassure her, but I realized how important it was for me to hear these things, process what I was hearing, and use this to build our relationship.

Rewind a few months . . .

It's become a tradition for my family to travel during the Christmas season to Florida, where my mother lives during the winter months, away from Chicago; she hosts our annual holiday party and no matter what I'm doing, or where I am in the world, I insist on going to Florida for that, to use the season as a time to reflect on what I am doing, on my intentions, and to remember what is important to me, namely my family.

Aunts and uncles and cousins and family friends made the trip that year, as well as my daughter, just starting out at Howard University. It was a time for all of us to catch up and to enjoy the mild weather in Florida, as opposed to some of the family shoveling out from a blizzard back in Chicago.

I forget how it came up, but someone made the comment, or asked the question, regarding kids, and whether or not I'd have more. The person making the comment—my aunt, if I recall—pointed out that I was still young enough to have more kids if I wanted, and maybe I should think about it. Actually, I had been thinking about it, and I said to my aunt that I'd love to have more kids in the future, depending on the situation. I wanted to be married, or at least partnered, and, at that point, I didn't see myself in a long-term relationship anytime soon.

Anyway, the conversation was light and funny, not at all as serious as perhaps I'm making it sound. But then Omoye spoke up, raised her voice a little bit, and objected. I couldn't have any more kids, she said to me, because if I did, then the new child or children would get the love and attention that she didn't receive. I heard Omoye loud and clear. It was the first time I caught a glimpse of my daughter's pain, and the degree to which she strongly felt it. I admit that in the moment, I wasn't entirely sure how to respond to Omoye. I think everyone sorta laughed it off, not to dismiss her feelings but to put a little positive light on what was a true feeling. We were all a little tipsy, but there was no mistaking Omoye's feelings on the matter of my having more children, and for just a few seconds, it felt a little awkward in my mother's house.

The party continued, and everyone had a great time. It wasn't until later that night, and in subsequent days, that I really processed what had happened, and wondered where it had come from. At first, I blamed it on the liquor (as we all do from time to time, I imagine).

But I felt a little worried. How long had she felt this way? And in what circumstances would she feel comfortable to talk to me? And most important: If she felt this strongly about this one thing, about the *possibility* of my having more children, then what else was on her mind? What was she not telling me?

Turned out the feelings expressed in that late-night call had actually begun to come to the surface during that holiday evening.

A few months after the call Omoye was home with me in LA for spring break, and though I don't recall how the conversation started exactly, we picked up from the late-night call and she more fully expressed herself. There was no alcohol; there were no other people or lighthearted jokes. It was a father and daughter having a conversation at least ten years overdue.

I got so defensive as our conversation continued. I didn't think Omoye was being unfair, and though she might not have had all the facts, she wasn't lying or trying to hurt me. But it's human nature, I think, to be a little defensive, when someone you love is explaining to you the ways in which they feel you've let them down. This is particularly hard to hear when it comes from your child. I wanted to defend myself.

But I knew this was a consequence of being gone so often for so long. You create this kind of vacuum, or void, where you're supposed to be in your respective family or household. And as time passes, your thoughts and feelings on matters aren't heard or reinforced. Something has to fill the space, especially for a curious girl who, on one hand, misses her father and, on the other hand, is angry, or perhaps hurt, by his absence. But I wanted Omoye to know that I wanted to be around, tried to be around as much as possible. I wanted Omoye to acknowledge me as a "good father," which felt then like just another way of saying "not a bad father." I wanted her to acknowledge me as a man who tried to do right by her. I wanted her to acknowledge my love for her, that it existed and it was true.

The more we talked, the more it became apparent to me that I was being not only defensive, but also a little selfish and self-centered, too. It happens so easily, to put myself at the center of a conversation that might not reflect me in a good light. It feels like being on the witness stand, I think, pleading your case, making your points of view known so that there is no confusion or misunderstanding. But this implies a little guilt, too. Isn't that what it's about when you're being defensive? That somebody's words hit up against something true, and it stings, and maybe you don't want it to be true, or to hurt, so you talk fast and dodge questions, or turn arguments against the person who made them. When you're feeling defensive, all of a sudden you're the most misunderstood person around. *Listen, you're not hearing me* or *I'm not saying you're wrong, but maybe you don't have all the information.*

Under these circumstances, it's hard to speak honestly and openly from a place of love. Perhaps it's impossible. Ego gets in the way of genuine communication and a real opportunity to begin the work required to heal wounds. I didn't want to be seen as a bad father, but as we continued our conversation I could see the damage I was doing, the manner in which I had prevented Omoye from achieving some progress. By focusing on myself, I had disregarded her feelings and her words, even if that hadn't been my intent. But my intent *was* to evade charges of not caring, of not fighting hard enough for her. My energy was spent on avoidance, not acknowledgement.

Instead of defending myself from everything, anything negative Omoye had to say about me, I started to listen, and rather than offer up excuses and explanations, I asked questions, with the goal being that I wanted to see the situation from her side of things. I asked her why she thought I didn't care. It seemed to her that I'd made a conscious decision to tour around the world too often, and as a result maybe I'd cared more about being a famous rapper than being her dad.

This hurt me, a lot, but in the moment it wasn't about my feelings. Still, I began to see the disconnect, the distance, between Omoye and me. Not because we were estranged, but because I only had one set of facts, one point of view, in rendering my own judgment about myself as a parent: "I am a good father." But I could see that ground had to be covered, that we needed to bridge some important gaps.

I told her that she had some points. Not that I didn't care—I did care, and it would've been a lie to suggest otherwise—but that at times, maybe I didn't care enough. Maybe I was selfish. Certainly I had to be, on some level, just as a circumstance of my work as an entertainer. I wasn't sure what I could've done differently. I thought about asking her, but this felt wrong. True, if someone you love feels hurt or let down by your actions, it's natural to ask, *Well, what can I do differently?* It's rational. And it's also selfish in its own right, too. As if it isn't hard enough for your loved one to be open and honest with you in regards to your behavior, and how they feel about it, now they have to come up with the answers for you, too.

It's one thing to hear a person out, to say *I'm listening*. And I wanted Omoye to know I was listening. But I needed to see her, too. I mean, seeing someone in your mind, thinking about the person, and understanding that your loved one is a full, whole human, complex and unsure, with shifting emotions and firm principles, just like you. By being honest with you, your loved one is *doing the work*, so it's super-important, I think, to see and respect where their effort ends, and where yours should begin.

When I first thought about writing a book on love, the idea itself seemed too big. Others have done it, of course: *All About Love* by bell hooks is a classic, and it guides my consideration of love's transformative nature. Love is a positive force in life. I've seen love reshape people's entire lives and outlook on themselves and others. The love of God, the Most High, adds depth to my very real and human life; regardless of being a celebrity, at heart I'm still that lanky Black dude from the South

Side of Chicago; I'm still that little kid who was a ball boy for the Bulls, who loved his mother, and loved his father yet was aware of his absence.

It seemed to me that in deciding to write about love, I had to ask myself a fundamental question: Would I focus on love's presence, or its absence? Setting one's intentions is so important, I believe, and I never start a project, whether it's a new album or a new role in a movie, without establishing intent. Love and intent are interlocked. What is the intent behind my desire to write a book on love? And what does it mean to write a book *on love*? Am I referring to love of God, love of self, love of parents and children, or of a romantic partner, or of community, with activism and with philanthropic work? What *is* love? What does it mean to me?

If nothing else, it means to let love have the last word in any situation, no matter the person. There's no other way to approach it than as an intentional practice, and it's okay to not know exactly what to do, or how to do it. There's no one clear way. It's more important, I think, to set the intention, to make it clear to myself. Saying *Let love have the last word* is not just a declaration—it is a statement of purpose, and it is a daily promise.

"To truly love," wrote bell hooks, "we must learn to mix various ingredients—care, affection, recognition, respect, commitment, and trust, as well as honest and open communication."

I first thought about these words in the context of partnered love, or even familial love—types of love that involve and are angled toward other people. But what about myself? To what degree am I caring and compassionate to myself, and how much do I recognize and trust myself?

I'm talking about self-love, but it's deeper than that. It's a constant adjustment, like tweaking the knobs to the board in the recording studio, trying to create the perfect sound— except, in the case of love, there's no end goal, no stopping point in the adjusting and tweaking. Love is a daily practice and it calls for us to step to it every day, to choose love every day, as though we didn't choose it yesterday, and the day before, and I think that's how it really works.

Because while it is important to remember what our loved ones did for us yesterday, how they stood by us, defended us, cared for and respected us, all of that would mean very little if today they choose to no longer love us, if they choose betrayal or infidelity or dishonesty. Love is a positive and transformative force only if we elect to refresh it every day, to regenerate and recycle it through our lives.

Thinking about it this way, saying *I love you* has far more weight, and should be treated carefully. Me personally, I am hesitant to say *I love you* too soon in the case of a romantic relationship, because while I might feel strongly toward the other person, and I want to be around that person, saying *I love you* is a different matter entirely. It's a declaration of intent more than a reflection and reiteration of emotion, though I don't think that's how we use the phrase in our everyday language. When we feel love, we say *I love you*. But if you think of love as a verb, an action, then the sentence becomes a promise for action, stipulating your commitment to that other person in the moment, in that day, to act with love, in love, anchored with clear and positive intent.

What I'm learning with Omoye is that the matters of love are easier said than done. I think it's because we're afraid at times. I know I sometimes fear vulnerability. It's emotional exposure, and we're all on guard, protecting our hearts, which, in thinking about it, seems a little silly. Life is all about living the best we can in a world that rarely makes complete sense to us, and to shepherd ourselves and our loved ones through the world while avoiding as much pain and injury as possible. But it's asking too much of ourselves to avoid pain. I love basketball, and I love working out. But this means that my body is in pain sometimes—a pulled muscle here, a strained tendon there—and this is only natural, expected. Why would it be different for our hearts, our emotional bodies?

We should care for one another as an act of love, as a way to express love in action, but loving other people comes with a price. Love never leaves us, but people do, and it hurts. A broken heart can feel devastating; it feels like grief, as though someone died, as though you're mourning yourself, or a version of yourself, gone from you forever.

Love is a beautiful and wonderful emotion that can simultaneously gut us from the inside out, so we keep it at arm's length, and perhaps engage love with some skepticism, with some distrust. I wonder how many people love their spouses but are, at the same time, afraid of the pain their spouses could cause and, with this fear in mind, never quite commit all of themselves to their marriages and partnerships, as if they're protecting a little bit of themselves in a jar inside a bomb shelter, just in case things blow up.

I'm not judging; I'm sure I've acted in a similar manner. But if everyone is protecting themselves and guarding themselves, then who is actually extending themselves to foster love? How does love present itself in a world designed for action—things in this life only happen when we get up and decide to make them happen—when so many people are so afraid of being hurt that they engage in behavior that *looks* like love, that mimics the ins and outs and ups and downs of love, but is perhaps not love at all, but something else entirely?

How do we trust in the love that is brought to us by others? And how do we trust in the love for ourselves? And how do we love God, our Creator and the One who looks to us to live in a manner representative of Him, when we trip ourselves up on love down here, on Earth, among our spouses, our children, ourselves?

. . .

All these questions started to swirl in my head when I thought about this project and how to best approach it. At first, I thought of love as though it were a wheel, with a number of spokes attached from the center to the outer rim of the wheel, and each spoke representing an aspect of love: love of self, of God, of family and children, of romantic partners, and of the community, the world at large. The wheel is designed for motion, of course, for forward movement, so it makes sense that love would be a wheel that allows one to progress and move ahead in life. But it's deeper than that, I've come to realize, but only when I started to write and realized that love is far more all-encompassing than I'd ever imagined.

It's not impossible to parse out and compartmentalize love, to chop it up and put the pieces in little boxes with labels outside of them: God, Family, Lover. But is that how we really love? Do we open one box of one type of love while closing and shelving another? And is this the process, a constant opening and closing of boxes? Or is it a little more fluid than that, a little more nebulous and perhaps more difficult for us—for me—to understand?

For the purposes of a book, it probably does make sense to compartmentalize, to cut love up into chapters that can be skimmed, or read in whole, or skipped entirely. But that's not really a concept so much as it is a form; like, you might have a dope idea, but you still need to record the album.

Love can take many shapes, but it transforms depending on context, and it can become warped if we're not careful, if we don't investigate the love we have inside ourselves, investigate how it manifests itself through our actions, and *why* our actions and our words, when it comes to love, sometimes fall out of sync with each other.

. . .

I started to think about this for myself recently, as I continued to process everything that was happening to me and Omoye.

I've had to acknowledge some basic truths: I was not a bad father, but I could be a better father to her; no matter how much I loved my daughter throughout the years, the fact remains that I was often absent, and she has a right to feel a way about this, positively or negatively. It's not for me to say, but to respect and understand; whatever it is I think I give Omoye, however I think my love translates into action, something is still getting lost in that type of communication, where she has felt over the years that I didn't care about her. And it is selfish of me to reiterate to her with my words how much I love her when she calls for me to adjust my actions. Even if I say *I hear you* and *I'm listening*, I really don't and I'm really not, because if I were listening, I would shut up and figure out what my daughter needs me to do for her, then do it.

And then there's one other truth, something I think will pop up over and over again as I continue to write, this idea that men tend to perpetuate, the idea of *fixing* something. I know I've said it to Omoye more than once: *I want to fix this. Just be patient with me and I can fix it*. But fix what, or whom? Not every issue she brings to me *can* be fixed. We both acknowledge that as much as the past might still hurt her, it's the past, and neither one of us can travel back in time.

As much as I want to, I can't go back to when she was a baby, or a toddler, or a first grader, and undo some of my more selfish decisions, or simply just be around more often. And even if I *could* go back and fix things, Omoye would not want me to, because that's not why she told me how she felt, why she shared her pain with me. She doesn't want me to change everything, because then she would change, would become a different person. All she wants from me is to have a productive and honest dialogue, which is in itself valuable.

Believe it or not, most times it is enough to know that someone is hurting because of your actions—but I hate feeling help-less, powerless. I want to *do* something, anything, to help my daughter, to help anyone I claim to love.

Just like when Jay Dee, rest in peace, lived with me in Los Angeles before succumbing to his illness and I watched that brilliant man, that musical genius, slowly deteriorate, knowing there was nothing I could do to help him. Except—I did help him, in some way, by spending time with him, laughing and talking with him, seeing and hearing him, by acknowledging him rather than running away, concerning myself with his health, his life, rather than feeling sorry for myself, making it all about me.

I want to give my daughter the world, but that's just a sentiment. I can't really give her the world, but I can love her better—yet that's just one aspect of my purpose here. Love runs through me and my entire life. It permeates my art, and yet it's clear to me now how little I have understood it. I love to read self-help titles and I speak affirmations. But as I am growing as a human being, I can see the other side of my life. I don't just want affirmations; I seek to understand.

Oftentimes music and art can express for us what we have not yet learned how to say in our everyday words.

—Dr. Angela Davis

———

've lived in Los Angeles for a few years now. I moved out west for a couple of reasons, including wanting to seriously pursue my acting career and put myself in the best position to succeed in that regard. Living here makes it easier for me to maintain a healthy lifestyle as well. I work out just about every day, and I try to squeeze in as much time on the basketball court as possible. When I'm performing, I give my all. I jump around. I sprint from one side of the stage to the other. It's important to give everything I got to the fans who have paid their hard-earned money to see me live. I take care of my body, and I'm mindful of what I put into it. The fresh juices and turmeric might not always taste great, but they help me feel better in body and in mind; feeling good physically means it's that much easier to feel good emotionally or, at the very least, to be present and aware when I'm not feeling at my best. When this happens, I take the time to care for myself, to do some of the things I love to do when I need to relax, whether that's enjoying a good dinner with friends and family, watching a movie, or just relaxing in my home.

Another thing I like to do: Get in my truck and drive. I turn the music up and I roll the windows down. The fresh air breezes through, and the big sun pours its light on me. It feels warm; I breathe a little easier and focus on the moment, the road.

Recently, I got in my truck and decided to play one of my favorite albums, *A Love Supreme* by John Coltrane. It's one of those perfect albums that come along every once in a while; when Coltrane plays those opening notes, I just feel at ease. I don't know how else to put it. It reminds me of the power of music, of art in general, and every time I play the album, I think about a man driven by his genius to achieve through his music a higher level, his higher self. He kicked drugs and alcohol, and dedicated himself to his craft, his spirituality.

I wonder what inspired him; I wonder what inspires all of us to transform, to evolve, to become better versions of ourselves. Yes, despite our flaws, we are good enough as we are now, and sometimes in our daily lives we forget that there's nothing inherently wrong with us in the moment. But we can always do better, be better, to ourselves and to our loved ones, and to the world.

I make my way through Los Angeles, taking the off-ramp from the freeway en route to one of my favorite destinations. Well, not so much a destination as it is a stretch of road, the Pacific Coast Highway, in the direction toward Malibu. I can turn my head to the left and see the Pacific Ocean, clear and blue, like a sheet of glass reflecting the sky above. With Coltrane doing his thing, *A Love Supreme* blasting through my speakers, I try to clear my head and think things through. I think about Omoye and all the things she said to me. Like Coltrane, I want to do better, be better, reach for and achieve a higher self, and yet I'm down here on Earth, dealing with the real, so to speak, grinding daily and having to deal with all the stresses that come with living life. A lot of people depend on me, no one more so than Omoye, and no amount of money and fame can take away the anxieties, the fears, the doubts.

Love never leaves us because it flows through us, our lives, as direct descendants of God, the divine source of all love in humanity, forever and ever available to us to draw from and to steer and direct our actions, manifesting love through the things we do. People, on the other hand, leave our lives all the time. Even when I think about getting married one day, I remind myself that in a perfect marriage—loving and healthy and full of wonderful and memorable experiences—sooner or later, your spouse will leave you as well. *Until death do us part*, so it goes.

But even in divorce or breakups, just because two people part ways and decide it's best to move on separately, it doesn't mean that one or both people are bad, or not good enough. The reasons why a relationship ends are independent of your value as a person, which existed long before the relationship began, and still exists even as the other person exits.

Love never leaves us, but people do—and that's okay. Love is inseparable from people—it's literally a part of human nature to love, to be loved, and to desire such a thing.

But love, as its own thing, is so much bigger than just one person, one relationship or marriage. It's bigger than a father and his daughter. Omoye and I are just people. My love for her is, of course, different from the love I felt, and still feel, for past romantic relationships, just as it's different from my love for my mother, or my art, or for Black people. And yet, love is, at its core, the same emotion, the same way of living and acting in this world, no matter who receives it from us. How we love in one context informs how we love in another. It's like that red line on a map when you're looking at your phone, figuring out how to get from point A to B. You can trace the path with your eyes, your finger. It's all connected.

But unlike with maps in our hands, we sometimes get lost and don't know how to get back on track. We don't know where we're going. We lose sight of what we know to be true about ourselves, and, when engaging with our lower selves, we end up in darkness. It's less about how to love one another, although that's important, and more about how to acknowledge love as a way to live our lives.

We are all so afraid these days, every one of us, no matter where we live, or what we do for work, or who we love. We're scared of losing progress. We're scared for our children and the kind of world we're leaving behind for them. I'm sure if I ask my mother right now, she'll tell me about similar fears she felt at one point or another. Maybe she still has those fears now. But something is different about this moment in time.

Speaking as a Black American, I can't recall a time when there weren't fears of losing your livelihood through racist employment practices, or your freedom through mass incarceration, or your life at the end of a police officer's gun. Something else is going on now. I can't put my finger on it, and maybe you can't, either, but I'm sure you feel it, too.

So many more people in our country have become addicted to drugs. And on social media, with the fast-paced news cycle and so much information, true and false, flying around, it can feel like life is destabilized and ready to crack open and explode and take us all with it. As citizens of the world, we've failed to take care of our planet, and now, with a warming climate, we are faced with new challenges and a deeper fear that our home, our Earth, is in peril, and it is our fault.

All the problems in the world, even our everyday crap—

paying bills, caring for our kids, working for that new promotion, whatever—feel magnified, enhanced. I don't mean to preach. You know all of this. I know it, too, and it matters to me to try to help repair the damage. It's part of my purpose, I've come to realize. It's bigger than record sales and box office numbers. For me, it's about going into prisons across the country, talking with the men and women who live there, hearing their stories, acknowledging them as humans, despite their present condition.

And in doing so, I don't believe I'm fixing their lives and curing them of all the struggles and stresses that plague them. But I do believe in the present moment, in what can be done *here* and *now*. In that present moment, I choose love.

No, I don't know the person, so I can't say I love them as I love my daughter, my team, or my "fam" from back home in Chicago. But I can act in love. I can give time just as easily as I could ignore them, walk right past them. I could be that dude. But I choose to do better, be better. I want to help others make that choice, too, in the here and now, the present moment—the only moment we've got and can depend on. The past is gone but not forgotten; the future is unknown and not promised to us. Each second we breathe is all we have and can claim for ourselves as *for us*.

It seems now more than ever before, there are a number of stories out there that deal with young Black men and women being shot and killed by the police, whether on television or in films. And at times, the subject matter can feel repetitive and cliché, without offering up fresh and human perspectives, diverse and nuanced and complicated, that can continue to illuminate both the prevalence of the shootings themselves and the real effects these killings have on everyday people, on family members, on members of the Black community, and on law enforcement officials as well. But I received the script for *The Hate U Give*, written by Audrey Wells, directed by George Tillman Jr., and based on the novel of the same name by author Angie Thomas. When I read the script, I felt there was more to the story than a depiction of yet one more Black person shot by a cop. The story is about a Black family, a community, and how a young lady deals with her life and identity as she maneuvers through the world to survive and hopefully thrive.

I related to so much of the story, especially in seeing how much young Black people today have to do to make it, just to give themselves a fighting chance each and every day; I understood the mentality behind "code-switching," and the story gave viewers a little insight into the experiences of young Black women, Black families, and Black communities. Everything about the script dove deeper into the experiences of us as a people, into our dynamics between one another, and our humanity.

After I finished the script and read the novel, I was excited for an opportunity to be a part of the project. What particularly interested me was the character Carlos, who is the uncle of the protagonist, Starr Carter, and a police officer himself. We as people who are standing up for young Black people who are being shot by the police rarely think about what the police officer is dealing with on a daily basis; we rarely take time to hear from him. And I think one of the greatest mechanisms toward resolution and healing these situations is to hear from everyone, to come to the table open to understanding.

I thought my taking on the character of Carlos was a chance for me as a human being to listen more to what police officers are dealing with, specifically Black police officers. Roles I take on give me a chance to be more in tune with human beings, to walk in other people's shoes, to have more compassion and understanding for their experiences. I thought it was important to hear the side of a Black police officer, who first and foremost is a human being. If we continue to be on opposite sides, there will be more young people losing their lives.

I think about the fact that Jordan Davis's mother is still missing her son every day; Sandra Bland's family is thinking about her every day. We can talk about these deaths in a distant, abstract way, or with a cool, informed mind, but we cannot discount the tragic and inhumane manner these families are impacted by their losses, day after day, year after year. And to remember the tragedies and their consequences is to activate a daily commitment to resolution. In my experience, one of the more impactful ways to effect change is to get people from all arenas in the same room, not just to talk but to strategize how to do things differently, how to treat people differently, and how to revise policies and laws with real-world impact on all of our communities.

. . .

The wind whips around as I drive up the coast. Text messages are vibrating on my phone, but for now I take this time for myself and I don't respond. The messages can wait while I enjoy the day, the present moment. New verses appear in my mind, as they always have throughout most of my life, the Most High and the world that I inhabit both inspiring me to work. I start rapping to myself. Even though I'm paying attention to the road ahead of me, watching my speed and the cars driving past, I enter into a familiar zone where I begin to freestyle.

When I'm freestyling I feel very connected to God, to my life, and I try not to disrupt the flow by thinking about the next word. There's no need for me to involve my thinking mind in this process because it's wholly creative. It's like surrendering myself to the moment, to the words that come out of my mouth. I trust in these moments that my heart and the creative part of my mind will guide me to a good place.

Art has this way of taking us back to where we came from, to our former selves that feel familiar yet strangely distant from us. Who I was when I was twenty years old is a completely different person from who I am now, yet the twenty-year-old *was* me. I lived those moments. Then, as I do now, I wanted to be present for everything. Back then, I had a child's idea of what love meant to me. But now I understand that love is far more complex than I first imagined, and I understand better its impact on our lives.

Living in love, with love as our daily driving force, can transform and affect lives. There is no other way to save ourselves from anxiety and fear. From a single point in time, and with belief in one human emotion, granted to us by God, we can chart for ourselves a new path, a new way to live in our modern technological world. Everything feels so fast these days, even time.

But maybe here, in this space, with these words, you and I can slow things down, carve out time and space for ourselves on the Pacific Coast Highway, and wonder, with wonder, what kind of world we can conjure in our imaginations. With love, maybe you and I can begin the slow work of rediscovering our value as individual people, as a community. Our higher selves call us forth to do this work. I acknowledge the call.

PART TWO

It isn't the mountains ahead to climb that wear you out; it's the pebble in your shoe.

—Muhammad Ali

———

Love is beautiful. It amplifies human life and nature. Those who create with love know and have revealed to themselves the light of the world. In dire circumstances, some of the world's most beautiful and poetic art has been created by people moved by love. Creating art is so inexact. What the mind imagines and what is actually created are two different things, and the artist is often frustrated by the separation. But love is worth the effort. The effort itself is love.

A personal transformation goes beyond the surface, that is, beyond how we present ourselves day to day. A personal transformation is a new worldview, a change in how one views oneself within the world, the adoption of a new perspective.

It's radical and difficult to do, with no guarantee that it'll actually happen; a personal transformation might contain milestones and goalposts, some quantifiable way for the person to measure real changes within themselves, as well as in their daily life, but transformation doesn't simply stop. It is an ongoing process.

In the liner notes to *A Love Supreme*, John Coltrane wrote: "As time and events moved on, a period of irresolution did prevail. I entered into a phase which was contradictory to the pledge and away from the esteemed path; but thankfully, now and again through the unerring and merciful hand of God, I do perceive and have been duly re-informed of His OMNIPO-TENCE, and of our need for, and dependence on Him."

Turning to God requires one to turn over one's doubts to God, to hand them over, to trust in each and every decision made if, in looking back, the decision was made with clear in-tention and with love in mind. There is no need to fear failure when trusting God, when living life in love, with love, when living by love.

That feeling of doubt, that lack of certainty, is in our daily lives, in our inability to perceive the future, to see oncoming danger before it arrives. Doubt freezes people, myself included. I sometimes think I underestimate my own cynicism, the more I think about it, the more I consider love and what it can do for people's lives, and my own.

But everything I know about love comes back to being vul-nerable, exposed, to just be and say whatever is necessary, so long as I am true to me. Everything else is outside of my control. John Coltrane understood this, too, I think. His later music eventually alienated many fans who wanted the smoother, more controlled sounds of his early work, his pre–*A Love Supreme* recordings. And yet he kept going, he kept pushing himself. From all evidence, he was motivated by God, pushing himself closer and closer to God with every new sound, with every note played.

The song titles for *A Love Supreme*, then, perhaps take on a new meaning, or one more dimension. "Acknowledgement," "Resolution," "Pursuance," and "Psalm" now appear to me as a cycle of doubt and the manner in which love can defeat it through daily practice: first acknowledge the doubt, then resolve to overcome it, requiring pursuit, perhaps daily, and ending with a prayer, a thank-you, to God.

John Coltrane might have feared his own doubts, but stagnation was unacceptable to him. He could've continued after *A Love Supreme*, his best-selling album, to make the music that gained him a following. Instead, he veered away. It speaks to his bravery as an artist, and his commitment to his own personal transformation, his spiritual awakening.

John Coltrane was an artist bold enough to exclaim the truth: "A love supreme" says it all. He lived a short life and delivered before his departure a catalog of art for all of the world to listen to, and to enjoy.

All artists have to start somewhere. A template is provided, a road map of sorts for the artist to follow when first engaging art, and when in that love frustration is born—the result of the art looking nothing like what was first imagined in the soul—one way to ease the frustration, and therefore ease into practice, is to see how someone else did it, and to try it their way, if only for a limited time.

Love is never different; love is susceptible to inauthenticity when the person who wishes to engage in love has no idea what it means for themselves, if they haven't discovered the love language, the words that accurately reflect their particular truth.

The good thing, however, is that love is a practice: diverse and duplicative effort, repetitive and concentrated work. Love can be refined. Much like art, love can be expressed creatively and outside the bounds of what is generally expected and has been previously witnessed.

It took the removal of drugs from his system for John Coltrane to hear his art, his specific and unique sounds—the inner visions and workings of a human expression never fully revealed to the world, and perhaps to the human himself. Returning to the liner notes of *A Love Supreme*:

"During the year 1957, I experienced, by the grace of God, a spiritual awakening which was to lead me to a richer, fuller, more productive life. At that time, in gratitude, I humbly asked to be given the means and privilege to make others happy through music. I feel this has been granted through His grace. ALL PRAISE TO GOD."

A *spiritual* awakening which led John to a *richer, fuller, more productive life.* Fifty years later, he continues to speak for himself, and his work reverberates still with new dimensions to explore in *A Love Supreme*, regarded by many as his masterpiece, myself included. *A Love Supreme* is one of the greatest pieces of music ever recorded, and one of the best jazz albums of all time. *A Love Supreme* is a superior work of art, the work of a genius who applied both talent and practice to his craft, yielding otherworldly results.

. . .

Matters of the spirit rise above the world, the physical world being just one part of our reality; the spiritual is the other, and to exist in any meaningful way in life, both should be engaged. Love is the way, the conduit from the spiritual to the physical, from soul to mind and body; to speak of love is to speak on a spiritual plane.

I tend to think this is a spiritual battle, a back-and-forth between the material and the divine. God's love comes first, but without love for myself I could've never opened myself up enough to understand and accept God's love in my life. It started with me. I had to first hear the word in order to become activated, moved, to manifest the word through my body, my art, my own words. Does God love you when you don't love yourself? Do you need to love yourself first? Or is the love for self always there, always inside of you, since the first second you come into the world?

First present in motherly arms, love has to be realized, again and again, as one matures. Over and over, we need new reminders that love is possible, and this does not mean we need new people to love us. We only need to see ourselves newly, I think. The more I love myself, the deeper I dive into the love, the more it feels inexhaustible, and though perhaps because it is incomprehensible it is also beyond my appreciation, the experience of love is felt, and therefore remembered. It's like muscle memory but throughout the entire body, a full-being recall of the deepest and most influential of our emotions.

Love is everyday life and experience. Without the day-to-day struggling of loving other people, ourselves, our gods, love itself remains a remote idea, something to hypothesize about to make ourselves sound like we have it together. Few people appear successful to us more than those who've somehow cracked the code and figured out how to live in love. It's about getting out of your own way, I imagine. Avoiding any opportunity to create a new problem for oneself, maybe. Without concrete information, a how-to that'll tell me how to do it, love is a thing to intellectualize, to consider, when I want to feel its full depth.

Ask someone who appears happy in love how they did it, what's their secret, and you'll find yourself unmoved by the answers. Doesn't matter what is said in response, because the advice given can't be applied to your life one-to-one, as if you're using someone else's map to move around, to find landmarks and sites that are important to someone other than yourself.

You have to make your own map. You have to be generous and bold, open and vulnerable to love; all the things I am not sometimes. I'm selfish and cautious, closed off and cold; I want what I want when I want it, like a child at times, but I figure if I can point to the problems, this is the first step, to identify with clarity the issues before me. Whether I do anything to remedy the situation is another matter, equal and related but independent from identification, from seeing myself for myself. That's an act of love, and I think if I can cultivate it for myself, I'll be served all the better for it when it's applied to my next romantic relationship, as well as with my daughter.

Acknowledgement, in other words, is the key. It can open a door for you, and when you walk in, you'll see yourself and the people you love in whole new ways. You'll begin to be honest with yourself about who you are, and how you treat not only yourself but other people in your life. Sometimes we fool ourselves, and we fool other people, but sooner or later we have to get real and face the truth; acknowledgement can help us to understand the impact our actions can have, and when we're no longer confused—when we can start to see ourselves more clearly—we have a chance to finally let our higher selves shine through.

Ask yourself why you no longer believe in love. At the end of the answer, a face will appear in your mind. And with that face will come a flood of memories, emotions, and other sensations related to a past time and space in which you and this face, this other person, shared a thing called love. And in the middle of love, words were exchanged. Bodies came together. Ideas and plans for a shared life were drafted over dinner or in bed, maybe over the phone while on tour or in the back of your mind while facing the bathroom mirror, brushing your teeth, contemplating all the things that float in our minds, seemingly at random, in regard to our many desires. And in the end, it's all a risk.

We are fast to proclaim our imperfections in the wake of expectations. We see imperfection in ourselves: not just the way we are, or the way we should be, but the way we could be if we behaved in a way that would betray our lovers—if we just cared all about ourselves, in other words.

Some might call this freedom, or liberation, and anything that restricts our ability to be whatever, whenever, however we wish, despite consequences or in complete neglect of them, impedes our notion of freedom. No one wants to feel chained, bound up by expectations, yet we do it to one another all the time. *I expect you to love me in this particular way in order to appease my need to be loved, and I'll do the same for you; I'll do what I can to meet or exceed your expectations, even though they might run counter to who I am as a person.* Then again, who am I . . . as a person? Do I know myself? And if I don't, then whose opinion of myself should I most trust?

Often, we turn to our parents. My mother raised me with certain ideals, reinforcing not just a love of God but a love of art, of education, of fairness and equality, of personal responsibility, of a deep inner strength, the kind we need when we are in pursuit of the things and people we love and desire the most. She instilled in me a sense of self-esteem and self-respect, two things that have served me in every facet of my life in the forty-plus years I've walked the Earth. She gave me the tools to love myself, and I think I honor her well in that love, in how I regard myself, and how I am regarded by the world. But I also know not everyone sees a person in the same way all the time, least of all do we see ourselves that way.

One day, I like myself; the next day, I don't particularly care for myself, and I feel a sense of shame and a sense of duty to correct whatever I perceive to be wrong in me. I think this has had positive and negative effects on my life in love. That sense of duty fosters ambition, but it also can create a wall between me and the people I care about the most.

I wake up some mornings and feel like I can do it all, be it all, conquer every fear and meet head-on any challenge that persists from the night before. Whether or not I'm actually successful is another matter, but at least I feel this way, and when I do, when I feel empowered, I think I can do anything. And if you love someone who believes they can do anything, you might wonder what purpose you serve in their lives, if any, besides being the safety net to catch them when they fall down, but who wants to wait around just to pick up the pieces? What kind of love is that?

This is, I think, my expectation of people, that they'll be okay with my coming and going, my flying around the world, my freedom not only in the world but in my being, so long as I return to them, at some undetermined point in the future.

Conscious decisions to live a life powered and influenced by love come first from a deep and sincere commitment to earnestness, and this comes about only through a kind of surrendering, to trust completely in the unseen and the unknowable.

There are times I do not believe at all in my capacity to love someone, anyone, because I tend to feel flawed, burdened by indecision, if only in certain strict aspects of my life. Career-wise, I know what I want to do, and I go after it, and sometimes

I succeed and sometimes I don't, but in this respect the decisiveness is clear, perhaps mechanical, certainly dependable.

When it comes to my daughter, I'm not so clear. Yes, I love her—it is true and absolute. And I could express that love in a myriad of ways, through song or with action. I could find a way to communicate to her my expression of love, I suppose, through my "love language," but that's a one-sided view. Where is she in this exchange? Where does she get to say, *I need this-and-that from you*? And this is the other side of expectation. Though expectations from other people can weigh heavily on us, and even make unfair demands on our time and energy, the expectations themselves are not wrong. There should be a space in each relationship for expectation to be voiced, then deliberated. It should be discussed openly and in good faith, without one person trying to get one over on the other person, without us trying to gain something we want just for ourselves.

These types of conversations are the most difficult to have, which means they're the most important, the ones we need to have. They require vulnerability and intimacy, two areas that are problematic for me, personally, because I don't want to give anything up.

Once again, I was driving along the Pacific Coast Highway; it was an early Sunday morning. The beautiful sky caught my attention, and I listened to music, looking out for songs

I could potentially play for a DJ "contest" some friends and I had planned to do soon. Suddenly, "Zoom" by the Commodores started to play. "Zoom" was my cousin Ajile's favorite song. Ajile Turner died in a motorcycle accident in Brooklyn back in 2009. I thought about him immediately as I heard the lyrics: "I'd like to greet the sun each morning/And walk amongst the stars at night/I'd like to know the taste of honey in my life." Memories of his life flashed and disappeared in my mind. Ajile's spirit is never far away from me, but "Zoom" helped me feel especially close to him.

I thought about the greatness of life. The song made me appreciate the connection between music and life. At that moment, I loved how much music creates in my life, as a listener and a creator. I loved and cherished the time I had with my cousin while he was still alive. And I loved life, being alive, and having the opportunities here on Earth to effect change. Life is a journey we go through to figure things out, to discover, and being in moments of peace and happiness; of course, there are the moments of anger and anxiety. And as I listened to the song and felt a moment of peace, I also appreciated and saw the value in experiencing a full range of emotions. I understood the importance in being open to all the moments and having the courage to face them. All of this because of one song.

As I worked on the playlist for our DJ contest, digging into songs I hadn't heard in years, I kept having these flashbacks and connections similar to what happened with "Zoom" and Ajile. Chicago house music brought back memories of friends I grew up with, and the parties we'd like to go to and hang out at. I played "Be Alright" by Zapp, which literally took me back to memories of my time at college. I was dating my girlfriend at the time, who I met when I was still in high school, and I used to make mixtapes and write letters for her. Rediscovering the music helped expand my love for music; it served as a reminder of music's ability to generate positive feelings in all of us.

During this past year, I've been in the space of creating new music. I've enjoyed the process, the collaboration, the fun; there is truly divine creativity, where you don't know where the music is coming from as you're creating, and when you listen back, you can't even take all the credit for the creation. It's as if the music is given to you; your job in the moment is to be open and be ready to produce, or translate, what is given as it comes. I haven't felt this free musically since I worked on the album *Like Water for Chocolate*, released back in 2000. The connection between then and now is the clear and purposeful intention of creating music for no other reason than simply for creation itself. To work in this manner is to work in concert with love.

It's important to open yourself to this creative space, this form of love, where many people often tend to feel closed off and full of doubt or self-criticism. World-renowned dancer Martha Graham put it this way: "It is not your business to determine how good it is nor how valuable nor how it compares with other expressions. It is your business to keep it yours clearly and directly, to keep the channel open."

In art, I think it's being confident, or knowing that it is a divine expression; in either case, you're removing yourself and allowing it to come through you. In this way, there's little room for judgment; it is simply allowing things to flow through you, and there's no time or opportunity to criticize or doubt what comes. When you are creating, you should be aware of the divine expression, so you become familiar with it, and recognize it the next moment it comes.

When that happens, confidence builds up, and this divine expression, this love, has some utility to it. It's not something to be "called upon" at any moment, like "Okay, flow through me!" There is a process; some preparation is necessary. You have to "get into" that space, so to speak; for me, it's knowing I'm about to enter the studio to record or, again, I'm listening to music as I drive around, which helps me get into the space necessary for writing lyrics.

You can't help but become comfortable with vulnerability, and with the setting aside of your ego, if only for an hour or two, as you receive this flow, this expression that, for some reason beyond your comprehension, has chosen this moment to come forward and has chosen you to help manifest it into the world as art.

How is this not the energy behind what we call "love"? Creating music is an opportunity to see love new every time.

The purpose of life is not to be happy. It is to be useful, to be honorable, to be compassionate, to have it make some difference that you have lived and lived well.

—Ralph Waldo Emerson

To be loved is to be seen, and when it comes to faith in God, we hope we are seen by the divine, that we're not forgotten, left down here to figure it all out for ourselves. And when a human rests their eyes on us, sees us, our one, individual, and unique body among a sea of bodies in a party or on a city block, we feel activated, brought forth, chosen. More times than not, we just want to be seen, recognized, and cherished. We do not want to be ignored, for real.

Love dims in the shade of dishonesty, which eclipses what should be everlasting and inexhaustible light, as from an immortal source, a Godlike force that binds together everything in this world, in this life, despite how we might feel about it, and in spite of what we believe. There are consequences for all of our actions, and when we are dishonest we can never fully know the extent to which we've inflicted damage to another person's life and sense of self, and their sense of us as people to be trusted.

We never know how or in what manner it'll happen, but one day our loved ones will need us. It can be a simple thing: a late-night text message, an invitation to attend an event or dinner. Dishonesty derails any opportunity for real growth and connection between you and another person, between you and God, and between you and yourself. With dishonesty, there is bad faith. The rules of the game keep changing, and the advantage is always in favor of the liar, of he who is going out of his way to disrupt and disturb what should be a peaceful time and space, a simple yet wonderful moment.

Partnership is, for me, a worthy goal to attain, but I want it to be right, and with the right person. That I don't have it now only means that the past situations were not right for either of us, which doesn't absolve anyone of any decisions that were made, or of dishonest words and intentions. It's just that— when things end, all of the arguments, the disagreements, the recriminations, and the blame, all of it seems less important, maybe because it's too late to change things for the better.

The love is gone, and something failed to live on; it's a time for mourning, but usually I try to move on as quickly as possible. I dive back into my work; I write my songs, and I pursue my roles; I become more interested in my own daily life, in part because the work never stops, and in part to pass the time, which, I think, we all do when we feel like something is missing.

Never one to sit down and wallow, I try to get back up and live as though I'm not missing a thing. I suppose I am not, the more I understand myself, the more I am honest to myself about who I am, and what I want. There is a level of freedom I have difficulty giving up for love, for anyone, even family. I don't want people imposing on my time, and I don't like having my space disturbed. I like living alone. I like being able to hop on a plane and go anywhere in the world. I like feeling free in my movement, in my days.

I wish to make space in my life for love. But I don't want to lose myself. I don't want to make that long climb back up the ladder to myself, my own light, to get reacquainted, alone, ashamed, rejected. Nothing but questions. What if I hurt her? What if I can't be true and honest, and if that's the case, why would that be, if I love her? Why would I lie in love? Why would I hide in love? What's wrong with me? Am I unlovable? Am I flawed? Can I trust you? The aforementioned space, can I maintain it? Can you afford it? Do you know? I don't know if I can afford it or float you on credit just to have you here, a let's-wait-and-see situation, I can't do it anymore, I need to know. Is there a space for us to ask questions of each other, up front? Equal effort, in consideration?

Love, I've been told, is all about making compromises with other people, in the name of finding some common ground, some space where people can agree on what to do next, and how to treat each other, the expectations of a loving relationship.

. . .

Once, in the White House, I was talking to our former first lady Michelle Obama about relationships. (Just a normal, everyday situation, of course!) She insisted that I would have to make compromises in finding my ideal partner—this, after I told Mrs. Obama some of the qualities I was looking for in such a person. Who am I to disagree with Mrs. O? She was right in that there is no perfect person for anyone, that you have to take the good with the bad when it comes to dealing with other people, particularly in a romantic relationship.

But I am beginning to understand that compromising *myself*, to become inauthentic, to live and exist as something other than who I am, isn't love, and such a compromise is filled with dangers and pitfalls. It leads to resentment; it leads to unhappiness; it leads, eventually, to that feeling of losing oneself, compromising who you are and what you want out of life to such a degree that you render yourself unrecognizable. Fracturing oneself like a broken mirror, leaving oneself in pieces, and rendering one's reflection unidentifiable and unknown. No wonder we often exit love affairs feeling as though we've lost pieces of ourselves; in some ways, we do.

There are degrees, in other words, to personal transformations; they can happen without compromise, or with us making so many compromises that the transformation can have an adverse effect on our lives and identities.

The moment terrified me. When I first held my daughter, I felt immediate love at the sight of her, a unique moment in my life, one that I haven't felt again since. And whether at that moment or later, eventually the fear arrives, the doubt that you know what you're doing—and if it's your first child, chances are you really don't know what you're doing. In love, fatherhood is no different than a spiritual awakening, or a romantic affair; no matter the dimension, love requires daily practice, and commitment, and effort; love is felt, yes, but it isn't self-sustained just because of the biological bond between parent and child. Everything in love requires work. Everything.

. . .

In order to transform my life in love, with love in my mind and soul, I must start with loving myself fully. Speaking of the order of things, and what comes first, my relationship with myself predetermines what I'm willing to accept from other people, and what I'm willing to reject in the name of love. This is not to say, for example, that if a lover is violent toward me, such behavior is my fault, that I brought it on myself. No matter how much I truly love myself, other people can still deceive me, show me only one side of their personality, or a false personality, only to reveal their true, violent selves later on, blindsiding me. But loving myself, engaging in this daily practice of loving myself, will better prepare me to identify love in other people, and will also help me spot those people I would be better off avoiding altogether. A life lived with love remains an imperfect one, but such a life would be uncompromising in love, authentic, real, hopeful, and progressive toward the future.

Loving myself in this way would create the foundation needed to love another person, again without compromise; it would reveal to me over time truths about my personality, my nature, the needs I have, the wants, as well as the negative things I can work to heal; and once I know these things about myself, I can communicate them clearly to another person; and vice versa, if they, too, love themselves and work the ongoing process, if they practice love daily.

It's not selfish to think of love in these terms—love is not selfish; love is not to be confused with excessiveness and ego, or with a need to take and take from people, from life, without ever giving back, without wanting to repay love with love in return. Love is reciprocal; it is an exchange of our vulnerabilities and our higher selves in the name of transformation. bell hooks, in *All About Love*, reminds us:

"Giving is the way we also learn how to receive. The mutual practice of giving and receiving is an everyday ritual when we know true love. A generous heart is always open, always ready to receive our going and coming. In the midst of such love we need never fear abandonment. This is the most precious gift true love offers—the experience of knowing we always belong."

Give love; receive love—this exchange, this reciprocation, applies to yourself as well as romantic and familial relationships. When I begin a new romantic relationship, I admit I worry about repeating past mistakes, despite the warm feelings that rise up when new love begins.

I acknowledge the worries as things I should always ask myself—whether or not I'm moving too fast, for example, or am I continuing to take time to practice loving myself, as opposed to perhaps off-loading that work to a partner—but in all, I wish to enjoy happiness, which is always temporary, those high notes of new love that come down in time, or level off.

I wish for a romantic love that has moments of feeling as high at times. It can't always feel that way, but I want a romantic relationship where the thought of the other person, the memory of feeling those high notes, takes me back to those times that should never feel too distant, and with remembrance I feel once again the initial burst, the spark, that at times goes cold as relationships develop and mature. To really imprint these memories, I have to remind myself, in other words, to remain in the present moment.

In the past, an ex-lover would tell me about this one time that one thing happened, something funny or intimate, between us, and in thinking about it, I had no recollection of the event, no memory. I can be forgiven for forgetting things, just like other people. But the strange thing is, when a relationship ends, perhaps because the pain of the other person's absence is at its strongest, I am weirdly comforted by the memories of the good times, the early days, in part to remind me that despite the end of the relationship, love still exists.

Love is achieved by firmly deciding to love. It is a cycle. Love resolves itself, but I have to take action. My work is to identify my need for love and to provide it for myself, to continue my daily practice. The end of a romantic relationship should hurt; I find it hurts even worse when I can't remember its best times, the beginning; I feel doubly robbed of a deep, soul-enriching experience, even in the height of grief and heartache.

There's no getting that time back, so now I remain present, if only to remember the start of a new relationship, to experience and enjoy it fully, as I should every moment I live and breathe. Risk heartache by remembering every beautiful detail of the times spent with a person you loved deeply; though the pain will linger for a time, you'll be reminded of what you can provide yourself, always.

. . .

Every day, I want to feel like I am making progress in my life, that I'm taking on the challenge to grow. When I know there is a deficit in my life, some lack or perhaps an area that requires improvement from myself *of* myself, I feel like I am doing a disservice if I don't confront the challenge head-on.

Otherwise, how will I ever proceed? There is no progress without effort. That's not to say I always have the answers—on the contrary, it often feels like despite all that I've learned and experienced in my life, I know very little about life itself, perhaps even myself, too.

Some years ago, I spoke at Riverside Church in Harlem, at an event headlined by Dr. Maya Angelou. I was honored to be asked to speak at Riverside, given its cultural and spiritual significance to the residents of Harlem, of New York, and of the Black community in general.

I had some idea of what I wanted to say to the audience, and when it was my turn to speak I stood up and tried to speak from the heart, but I didn't have a set theme or direction in terms of what I wanted to say. *I'm not a public speaker*, I thought to myself. *I am a rapper and actor; these are my posi-*

tions, and they are indicative of my artistic life. And when I spoke, this was the perspective from which I shared my views on success, on purpose, on life itself.

At the time, I thought I was doing my best. I spoke for about ten minutes before Dr. Angelou held court and captivated us all with her wisdom. She spoke about humility, about being humble without walking with your head down. The strength we have as a people, along with the power of words, and taking destiny in our own hands throughout all our struggles—we are the children of the most resilient and powerful people. This was her message to us.

The energy inside Riverside as she spoke reverberated in the air; I could feel it tingling throughout my skin. Everyone in the church, from the speakers to the ushers, received her message as though it were an offering to be shared with the world, something we could take away and carry with us as we proceeded with our daily lives. Dr. Angelou spoke to our hearts and revealed to us our true nature, our spiritual power, in all its light and positivity, its ability to shine inside the darkest of spaces.

My mother was at Riverside that day, and when the event ended, we got into the back seat of the car. I don't remember what I was thinking at the time—maybe I was still buzzing off what Dr. Angelou had said, or perhaps I was feeling myself just a little bit, which is to say I probably felt pleased with myself and the things I'd had to say as one of the speakers.

Anyway, as the car pulled away from the church, my mother turned and said to me, "Rashid, you can do better. I think you have more to offer to people than what you just did. That speech," she continued, "could've been better. Did you hear how the other people spoke? Dr. Angelou? Listen to their words, then go back and listen to what you said. People couldn't walk away from your speech with anything that would matter to them, something for them to think about and have conversations with friends and family later on."

I immediately defended myself. "I was just coming from the heart," I said. And typical of me when I get defensive, I denied the challenge; or, that is to say, I tried to deflect the challenge away from me. "I'm not even trying to be a public speaker," I said, "so it's not even something I would or should work on. That's not my thing. I'm a hip-hop artist, not a speaker."

Excuses. I was offering excuses. True, I wasn't thinking of a career as a public speaker; but it was also true that I had been invited to speak at Riverside. I had been given a platform; I had been *asked* to be a public speaker. That was my role, my position, as part of my accepting the invitation to participate at the event.

To suggest that there was no need for me to give my all, to apply my best effort to the situation, because of a difference in labels or titles—rapper, public speaker, whatever—was like a shell game of sorts, where I was trying to quickly and deftly move and hide myself, and to be slick about it.

All just to avoid addressing my mother's point: If you have more to offer to people, and you are in the position to offer more, you should do it. It shouldn't even be a question. *It's your responsibility*, she was insinuating to me. *It's your responsibility to speak your best to the world when the world is listening to you and looking to you for answers, for guidance.*

More to the point, my mother reminded me of the importance of effort and applying myself. The idea of speaking to people and giving them something they can walk away with is less about appearing wise, or smart, or knowledgeable.

On the contrary, people are receptive and open to hear you when you speak from the heart, as I did—but they are more receptive to hear you when, in speaking from the heart, you speak with clear intent, with authenticity, with a sincerity that registers as a sign of someone truly wishing to give of themselves and their experiences to other people, through actions *and* words.

To give someone a word they can hold on to and use to potentially better their lives is to value their time. It is an act of love to speak with someone else in mind, to set aside ego and self-centeredness and to simply give with complete effort. To do otherwise is to waste people's time, and all one will have to show for it is a half-hearted effort.

All I wanted to do twenty-five years ago was make dope music that my friends would love, that other emcees would respect as real hip-hop, to provide a living for my baby daughter, now an adult woman, and to give back to those who raised me, my parents, namely, and more broadly my community: Chicago, yes, and Black people worldwide. All of that has happened over the years, but not without the struggle.

The idea of being a normal person living quietly and handling personal matters behind closed doors, where they remain, under lock and key, has something of a charming effect on me, though not enough to give up my current life and my freedom. I cherish the access fame has afforded me, especially since the time I decided to give acting a try, an idea that motivated me to push harder to meet the challenge, and yet also an idea that a few people, I know, did not support. They had their doubts. I understand; I had my doubts, too.

But they were outweighed by the need to try something new, to approach a creative pursuit as a challenge that could lead me to new and greater opportunities. It wasn't because I was bored with music. I love hip-hop. I love to rap. Real emcees in the world understand me when I speak of this love.

Here, I'm talking about art, but this love applies to other things as well. Religion, for one. And love of community. And love of self, which is, I think, the most complicated of the dimensions, because we so often keep shame in our hearts for the littlest things. For as much as we as humans are naturally inclined to change things, to look and perceive a thing and wonder if it's possible to improve it, including ourselves, we also think of ourselves as concrete and inflexible, incapable of change, perhaps unwilling.

. . .

I don't blame my father for anything, and I harbor no negativity toward him. Though he and my mother went their separate ways when I was just a baby, and though he lived in Denver while my mother raised me in Chicago, I felt his presence in my life.

As best as he could, my father reached through the wires during our phone calls and made me realize how love transcends geography, but not necessarily memory. While he was available, he wasn't always around, and it's hard to know for sure what difference it would have made in my life had my father lived in the same city as my mother and me, if he'd been a short bus ride away instead of a flight across a couple of states.

As for my mother, she did everything she could. She provided me with a good life, a well-rounded and active childhood. She made sure I was responsible in school, that I had a part-time job when I was old enough to work, and she shepherded me to college after high school. That I dropped out after a few semesters was all due to hip-hop, that love of mine, and the belief that I could succeed as a rapper if I committed myself to the work. My mother was skeptical, and rightfully so; I was dropping out of school and passing on a business degree for a dream, and not even a fully formed one at that.

There was no overarching scheme in mind when it came to music. I had an opportunity to rap, and I was already into the music, ever since I wrote my first rap back in 1984 at the age of twelve. I didn't want to disappoint my mother by dropping out of college, but I believed, and it was because of her that I believed in myself in the first place. Where else would such faith come from? My mother did all she could for me, and I watched her work. I paid attention to the hours she devoted to me, to our lives together in Chicago, and to her incessant looking forward, one eye toward my future. I saw the sacrifices, though perhaps I wasn't always mindful of them, or didn't always respect and appreciate them as a little boy.

But I was privy to the ways in which she loved me and cared for my well-being, and I never forgot. She told me herself how much she believed in me, how she knew I could be whatever it was I wanted to be. Truth be told, that did not include rap, or acting, or entertainment in general. My mother was, and remains, a practical woman, and her focus was to make sure I had all the tools I needed to make it on my own in the world when the time came. In the 1970s and 1980s, those tools undoubtedly included a college degree, and I think it was the desire of all Black families in America to send their children to college to earn degrees and to attain well-paying jobs so they could, as adults themselves, raise their own children to go to college, and so on. I had other plans.

Maybe my mother knew that from the start, or could see it in my ways; I knew I wanted to be someone who entertained people, but at the time I didn't know how, exactly, or in what way. Growing up, there were times I wanted to close the bedroom door and lock it behind me so I could shut out all the nonsense in the world and focus on things that brought me some pleasure, and that always included music, all the way from the time I first visited my father in Denver as a kid and riffled through his vinyl collection.

Thelonious Monk, Marvin Gaye, Gene Ammons. Some of these records were unearthed in the final weeks and months I spent with my father as his cancer progressed and his health deteriorated four years ago.

By that time, whatever lingering issues I had with the man with respect to my childhood, and the circumstances that led to him living in Denver, had been reconciled, or even quashed. There was no time for that, I figured; I wanted to spend every moment I could with my father, because I loved him.

He accepted himself, for all his imperfections, his flaws, but he knew he had wanted more for himself. He knew his capabilities were greater than what he had brought into fruition. Lately, I've had to go back and listen to his raps at the end of my earlier albums, spoken word poetry on subjects ranging from family to the state of hip-hop music, and I remember thinking, *These are really some things that will last forever. He marked the planet.* When I think of my father, I think of creativity, I think of hustle. I think of a soul with unfinished work.

I think of spirituality, strength, forgiveness, and about understanding the imperfections in all of us. My father never tried to portray himself as someone who was perfect. When he talked about his past, he was open and honest and he had this charm about him. Because there was truth in what he was saying, in who he was, and how he carried himself. Even though he had a lot of confidence, being a Gemini, he still was honest about his flaws. When I think of him, I think of the constant evolution of a man. I thank God for his spirit; I feel his spirit is still with me.

I remember the peace I felt when I went to visit my father at his apartment in central Denver. I took the elevator up to his place and when he opened the door, I noticed that his legs were swollen. He was wearing a burgundy robe, and he looked thin, his face sucked in. His eyes were still big, but they were red. Clearly, he wasn't feeling well, but the charm of his spirit was still present. Although I was sad because I knew how much he loved life, and I could see the illness taking its toll on him, I was also grateful I could just sit and talk with him, and listen to Gene Ammons. Omoye was there with me, and we all talked about the family coming together. He told me he wanted me to have his music, and he told me about some of the new stuff he'd recorded for a project I was working on. Then he got up from the couch and came back with a bracelet, and told me he wanted me to have it. There were different things that he had that he planned to give to other people. But he didn't give it to me like he was saying "goodbye," only—*I want to give this to you.*

It was a gold bracelet that had like an African type of thread to it. I carried it in my backpack a lot afterward. But after my father gave me the bracelet, he talked only about sports a little bit, and I remember the news was on, and I thought at the time, *Is my dad going to be here to see these different things in the world?* He talked about Obama at some point—he loved Obama. And he talked about how he wanted all of his offspring to be in one room together; that was something he'd always dreamed of and wanted to happen.

The last time I saw him, I was doing a show for Dave Chappelle in Denver, and my dad came through, and he always would invite a lot of people to the show, so he invited all these people. He invited the mailman, a guy from the bar, all his buddies, and people he'd promised something. It wasn't a great performance that night, but Dave Chappelle rocked it, and I was just happy to be doing something with Dave and my father. He came backstage with me and he had on one of his hats. When we came down after the show, he talked to me and Dave; people could see that he was sick, but he still was talking mess. And there was a warmth in his talk, too, you know; he invited people over and he was really nice and cool.

He was telling all of us how sharp Dave was, and how proud he was of us, and he loved it that we stayed true to what we believed in. And then he started talking about some of his music that he had worked on. I think that was part of his hope. When we talked about his work, it didn't feel like he was making the transition to death, because we were planning for the future.

My friend was talking to me recently about her grandmother, that she may die soon, and I said, "We have to stay in the present. There's nothing that you can do to control it, besides doing everything you can to give love and be there for her. Beyond that, you can't really worry about tomorrow—today, she's alive." And that's how I dealt with my father's cancer, knowing there was really nothing I could do to change his prognosis. All I could do was love him, and remain in the present with him, and continue to plan with him for the future, as long as there was a future. If I could call him at that moment, I called him, and we would be able to talk in the moment, one more moment.

Anyway, backstage at Dave's show he said, "Y'all always

flying over my head"—because we're always flying from New York to LA—"y'all always flying over my head." At that point, I valued our conversation even more. I always valued my dad's conversations because the talks meant something to both of us. When we were talking to Dave, I remember just cherishing and valuing the time and the moment. I was grateful that Dave and my father were able to connect. Dave had just started doing shows again, and to be a part of that with my father was really special.

Throughout my life, my father opened my mind to giving back to the community, doing charitable work, and activism work; he was a spark that inspired me spiritually, in maintaining a world perspective. He liked to say, "I named you Lonnie with the Christian name, and Rashid with the Muslim name, because I believe they both have the same love within them." This is why I feel a connection to Islam, and other religions as well, even though I identify as a Christian.

If he saw something, an injustice, he would speak up on it. He encouraged me to speak up but also to see things from a worldly perspective and to ask, *Where can I contribute something good?* We talked a lot about community; my community in Chicago kept me aware organically of my Blackness and of culture and bonding with the community, and showing support by going out to do things. My father was a direct source of activism; he would say plainly, "This is what we need to do"—but he wasn't always specifically political; he was also spiritual, social, his was a whole philosophy, a complete social consciousness. That phrase has been so twisted, especially with rap, like a "socially conscious" rapper, but when you're truly socially conscious, the key part is the spirit, the meaning, behind the idea or belief. Thinking of creative ways to better the world, to change the world, for example. With love in mind, looking at situations and thinking of unorthodox ways to shift them. My father was brilliant.

After Dave's show, I remember seeing my father pulling off in his truck for that last time. At a certain point, sometimes, when you know somebody is really sick, you think, *Well, is this the last time I'll see him?* We're supposed to stay in the present; I try to stay in the present, but I wondered, *Is this the last time?* I always had some hope he would make it through.

When I received the call weeks later, I was on set shooting an episode for a reality show. By that time, we had reached a point in my father's treatment where it became a mere matter of easing his physical pain and discomfort, and maximizing our remaining time together. And when he finally died—when I received the call on set—I felt at first relief for him, and thanked God for taking away his pain, which toward the end was becoming unbearable.

The very next thing I felt was disbelief. I had registered as fact my father's death—I knew it to be true the way I knew I was standing on set receiving the news via the phone I held and could feel in my hand—but those are just facts, data, more biographical information that can barely begin to accurately capture a life experience, especially the kind that one must endure and will always struggle to describe. But in the moment, I just couldn't believe that it had happened, even though I'd known it would happen, knew that it *had* happened. I was in shock. I didn't know what to do with myself.

I dreaded calling my daughter the most. She loved and was close to her grandfather, more so as time and the cancer progressed, and I made sure she came with me to Denver as often as possible to see and spend time with him. *What will she say?* I asked myself—her reaction was a foregone conclusion, yet I was just curious about the words she might say, the sentiment to be expressed, beyond the expected tears, the sadness.

What was more, I knew there was little I could do to take her pain away, as well as my own. In a world powered by love, death would not cause in us so much fright, which leads us to keep it at a distance and to not think about it, preferably for as long as possible—decades, if not centuries.

. . .

I ask myself if this world I seek, this one powered by love, is necessary, or even realistic—perhaps there is little need to make one up. A world where I made music with my father is a remarkable one. In thinking of my father, I realize that half the battle is learning how to carry our burdens, our suffering, with grace, discovering how to navigate our lives without becoming consumed by bitterness and anxiety.

Perhaps there is no other way to live. Perhaps this is all we can ask of love—to restore to us our dignity when life unravels and calls us forth to reconstruct ourselves once again, to rebuild amid destruction, to choose life and love every second there is breath in our bodies.

I've come to realize that there's a time to let go, to rise above, to transcend. As we become adults, we often repeat the decisions and perspectives of our parents. No matter how much we think we can do things better than our parents, we often stumble at the same spots and issues where they did, and it can have a humbling effect on us.

When humbled, a person tends to turn to God for assistance, for a word. God's love is the ideal love, because it never fades, and it is never withdrawn, taken back, because of misgivings, misunderstandings, or some change in feelings, the way people feel differently about other people as time moves forward. God's love is perfect, always present and abiding, firm, sincere, and constant. We are reminded by God's love of how far we as humans have to go in order to attain for ourselves such a bottomless and powerful force.

God never leaves us. God never lets us down. And God's love is unquestioned, our doubts notwithstanding. Have I ever doubted God's love for me? It's hard to say. Intellectually, I knew God's love was everlasting, but sometimes that was cold comfort during my difficulties, my problems, when all I could see before me were the challenges I had to endure and eventually master.

If anything had a limit, it wasn't God's love but perhaps my capacity to believe, or maybe there were times when things just got too difficult, and all I felt was pain and suffering, and I wanted God to love me and to take the pain away, not knowing that the pain and struggle themselves were the very tools I needed to overcome whatever trial presented itself in my life.

The art of love is largely the art of persistence.

—Albert Ellis

———

Love is complicated for everyday people who wish to live and experience the emotion, something they have been told—as all of us have—that without it, their lives lose some meaning or significance. What if I asked my friends and family if falling in love, as it is defined by them, was an important moment in their lives, an unforgettable point recollected now only through memory? I think many of them would raise their hands, say yes, and confirm for me what I always suspected, and perhaps felt intuitively: that love, for better and for worse, helped shaped them into the persons they've since become.

It's as if love rewires our brains; it's not that we forget our-selves—forget the people we think we are—but maybe it's too much to expect of ourselves, this need to reconsider ourselves, and to then conclude that not only is change necessary, but also inevitable. How you carry the fact is a personal matter, some-thing we all must figure out for ourselves. For me, I tried yoga, something that could change my physical experience to address my emotional one. It wasn't my idea, and the exercises didn't solve my problems, but I felt better physically, and in time, I could feel enough positive results in my overall well-being that eventually, practicing yoga was something I wanted to do.

The more I practiced, the less I was concerned about how I felt emotionally—heartbroken—though I'm not saying I didn't feel anything at all; what I felt seemed distant from me, at a remove that seemed to me *far enough*, a comfortable amount of space: I knew what I felt, and why, but I was no longer caught by my emotions, so long as I focused on something else, something outside of myself. I had no idea if this space was healthy or unhealthy, good or bad; it seemed necessary, is all I can say to it in retrospect.

We do what we can with what we have in our lives, the things we can place into our hands. If it's ten dollars, it's ten dollars, and that's it. I always figured I could pray for more, and so I do, but at the same time I cannot expect anything outside of myself to help me, not all the time. My friends, my boys from the South Side, they have lives of their own now; I'm counting the years in my head, one by one, like loose change, like the toll I didn't know I'd been paying this whole time since the day I was born.

You fall in love and at certain moments, things feel secure, reliable, *steady*; ten years later, you accept that it still hurts, it's a small stab of the thumb now, not the shooting pain, it hasn't been that way in years; but still—

Los Angeles is full of therapists; one on the street would stop me if they knew everything in my head and say, *Rashid, it ain't that deep, and you're not the only one*, but I'm not sure if I would believe them. Though, knowing me, I would stop my stride along the sidewalk to hear her out. It's rare I won't stop and talk with someone who steps to me or shouts me out.

It happens all the time now; it's white noise, background music, but not tuned out. I always ask the person for his or her name, and I go silent for a few seconds as they start talking. I would hear out the therapist, but I would be a little skeptical; I trust my mind, my heart, my faith in God, and my faith in people; I trust myself, in other words, first and foremost.

Rappers, for the most part, can be at their most honest when in the recording booths, or in front of crowds, microphone clutched in hand. It's not even like boxing or tennis, when you're on the stage by yourself, no hype men, just you and the microphone and your voice, the words in your head: there's no other opponent to defeat in the moment; you're just trying to express yourself freely.

That was the whole point of hip-hop music when it first started: A generation of Black American kids needed a new way to communicate, to say everything and anything that was on their minds, a common need to find and use one's voice, for real.

When I started rapping in the 1990s, I thought that was the whole point: speak your piece, but do it also in a dope way so your friends will give you props. Other things get in the way the longer you rap; this is true in entertainment and in life, but I try to keep hold of the faith, the reason why I started to rap, the first time I fell in love with the art.

For a time, I thought the art had turned its back on me, too. *Gaining love, losing love, regaining love, losing it again, new partner, old partner, ol' boy, new girl, significant other, someone I used to date, ex-lover, ex-fiancée, excommunicated, yes we used to smash, no I don't know where she's at, or who she's with, and I don't care, but I wouldn't mind if I knew anyway, speaking of keeping it real: How to live with love is how to feel about it, how you regard it from time to time, and it's not always a positive feeling; sometimes we feel hate, especially toward love.* It seems paradoxical, but it's been true in my experience, to resist the whole notion of love, the effort of trying to connect with another person, to establish harmony.

The best we can do is harmonize our lives with other people, whether with family or with a congregation, a classroom, a lecture hall, wherever people presently meet and must deal with one another. The only way you can harmonize with someone is by first knowing how you sound by yourself, as your own instrument, your own voice.

My voice is always with me, but sometimes I forget how it

sounds until I am alone and can think, or write, or veg out in front of my television and watch a movie, doing nothing, *being* nothing but myself.

Soon, I realize that I trust myself, and I trust in God, and I know God trusts in me—in these moments, it feels like I have everything I could ever need in the world. Other times, it's a little too quiet in my house, a little too much of me. There, on my white mantel, are photos of me on red carpets, or in mid-conversation with a famous actor or ballplayer; the framed art on the walls I chose myself; the books on the coffee table are mine, and I've read them all. I pick up the New Testament and flip to my verse:

> *Love is patient, love is kind. It does not envy, it does not boast, it is not proud. It does not dishonor others, it is not self-seeking, it is not easily angered, it keeps no record of wrongs. Love does not delight in evil but rejoices with the truth. It always protects, always trusts, always hopes, always perseveres.*
>
> *Love never fails. But where there are prophecies, they will cease; where there are tongues, they will be stilled; where there is knowledge, it will pass away. For we know in part and we prophesy in part, but when completeness comes, what is in part disappears. When I was a child, I talked like a child, I thought like a child,*

*I reasoned like a child. When I became a man, I put the
ways of childhood behind me.*

(1 Corinthians 13: 4-11, NIV)

. . .

I have no real memories of my parents loving each other, and our parents are the first lovers we observe in our lives. My mother and father had separated not too long after I was born, and after a series of events, altercations, my father relocated to Denver while my mother and I remained in Chicago. What I know about love, the little I admit to knowing, comes from my mother, a Black woman who raised me on her own, who, it felt, gave me everything I ever needed. She loved me enough for two parents, compensating as best as she could for my father's distance, which would persist throughout my childhood.

So if I do not have a clear memory of my parents loving each other, then I can at least recall two images: one of my mother loving me, and the other of the physical absence of my father, represented by a void, an image entirely blacked out as if taken from inside a black hole—absurd I know, but that's how deep the void goes. My father and I were close in the final years of his life, but in retrospect we didn't have enough time—for what?

To ask him about my daughter, and what I should do for

her, how I should help her. And to receive whatever advice he could offer about my love life, and where my blind spots are, if he could see them, when it comes to communicating openly and honestly and directly with women, in such a way that I do not hurt feelings or expose myself to unnecessary pain and drama. No one wants to get hurt or played, and yet it happens every day. I don't know why. The best I can do, given my purpose, is to appreciate love in all its facets, even in moments when it is betrayed, or it feels as such.

I know few examples of successful love. I admit my failure in imagining something greater and more rounded than the love of two strangers who then choose to have sex and children and hold hands and stroke each other's need to be desired; I thought to love was to desire, and it is, to a point. But I do not know if love is supposed to be a struggle; I know I do not struggle in knowing God's love for me. I understand that now, I see it now. The power of God comes direct from love. It is God's force, as old as the universe itself, and it is beyond conception of the human mind, a force that stretches out and over what we consider the human scale.

I am no prophet. I am a poet from Chicago. I am one man who dreams dreams and suffers from big ideas and wide vision in my mind, my head so high in the clouds. My mother dared me to dream; she loved me unconditionally, and wished for me to aim high, to keep my prayers angled upward so God may hear my desire to rise above the dark world and become reborn in light. It is unclear if it has happened; it might be happening now, as I write.

. . .

I'm not the same man I used to be, even just a few hours ago, a day ago, weeks ago, when I first sat down to write about love. Deep and serious reflection is required; now I understand why few people bother diving so deeply into love. It is painful. It is terrifying. The deeper you go, the more you learn about yourself, and the deeper you dig, the wider the hole, the more love you can contain within; it is not easy work. I feel dizzy at times; paradoxically, I become angry with myself for allowing in so much love, for digging deep, for bothering. It's easier not to care about people.

It's more likely that a child in our society will learn how to shoot a pistol than that they will learn how to love. What would the world teach this child about love in the first place? That it is not transformative. That one should be skeptical of love. That it's not possible to live as a lover, and that they must be on guard at all times. All that is required from them is a suspicion that the way we live on this planet is insufficient to sustain life as we wish to see it. We have nothing to hide but plenty to fear.

Alcohol used to be my vice, and I still keep it at a distance. My family history is populated with drunken men, and some drug addicts, too. It's difficult to see love in ourselves when we are in constant search for something that'll numb us from the pain. Why did I like to drink in excess at one time? It felt good to me. I could feel my stomach warming inside, and I felt woozy and light, and I wanted to feel more unstable, so I drank, and drank some more, becoming drunk, then resentful at myself for letting such a thing happen, for becoming so— messy, so—excessive with desire.

Was there a deeper pain I wanted to drown with the alcohol? Perhaps. Maybe I missed my father. All I want from the past is one more opportunity to see my father breathing and full of life, one more conversation between us, one more joke shared. From addict to activist, from ballplayer to poet—he had to get rid of the substances to see in himself the love he couldn't feel; the drugs and the alcohol had numbed him, kept him from facing and learning from his failures.

I would not ask for another man to have been my father if I had a choice, and I could never resent him. I miss him. Every day, I continue to learn how to live as a son without his father, a fatherless child. He let me down at times; he was selfish, as I was selfish with my daughter; the sins of the father represent a cycle we are destined to break or repeat, one or the other, and my work remains incomplete.

It was important for my daughter, in the name of love, to tell me how disappointed she felt, how heavy were the absences, and these were words I couldn't say in full to my own father. All I know is—he is gone, and I am still here, and I can still make a difference in my daughter's life, just as my father did for me later in his, despite the struggles that were dragged through my childhood, in some ways marring it, but not beyond repair. We made music together, my father and I. We created, and through creation, we reflected God, and love.

The greatest happiness of life is the conviction that we are loved; loved for ourselves, or rather, loved in spite of ourselves.

—Victor Hugo

———

Summer, overcast with occasional thunderstorms. I woke up thinking about all the things I needed to do, to say nothing of the flight that awaited. I couldn't remember dreaming, or falling asleep, and I would've preferred to stay in Los Angeles to continue talking with my daughter in pursuit of a resolution; I wanted to *do* something to help her and to alleviate some of my own guilt. After the late-night phone call and text conversation, I had dozed off. Reconciliation can't be rushed; it requires the patience to live and work with some emotional pain while revealing to the world only your smile. Life goes on, and other work has to get done.

For me, this can mean quite a few things now, not only performing and recording music, but preparing for movie roles, reading scripts and practicing, researching roles—sitting in an

AA meeting, for example, or shadowing a city police detective—as well as conducting interviews, planning documentaries, developing television shows, shaking hands at this gala, giving a speech at that foundation or awards ceremony. Unless I have some downtime to relax and reset, I travel to multiple locations a few days a week, every week. As much as I wanted to stay and talk with my daughter, I had a show to do in Colorado, then soon after that I had to record in New York, then head down to New Orleans, and finally overseas to London for a few weeks.

It's always been this way for me to some degree, on some kind of scale, whether big or small, whether flying first class or riding in the back of a panel van on tour from New York to California. Having to leave for work when my daughter needed me—again—only bolstered that feeling of guilt, transforming itself into a more urgent anxiety, the illusion of seeing myself as the good father removed and replaced by an accurate portrayal of the loving father who is never around, off to the next destination, chasing the next dream. It's my life, and I asked for it, I prayed for it, I worked every day to bring it out from dream to reality, but my daughter needs me—and I need to work—and on and on it goes, the cycle.

Aun scrambled around the house to check for any last-minute things I needed to pack before leaving for the airport; we were already fifteen minutes late. We brought the bags down and outside to an idling black Suburban, our driver waiting patiently behind the wheel; we had twenty minutes to get to LAX, when it usually took thirty from my home, not including traffic, southbound on the 405, which can either be clear and easy to drive or can be a parking lot jam-packed with cars. I asked the driver for the AUX cable and plugged it into my iPhone.

I was working on a new album, and I still had some verses to write and nail down, so I hooked my phone up to the stereo to play a couple of beats from my friends and collaborators Karriem Riggins and Robert Glasper, one of which was meant to be a remake or a cover of "Optimistic" by Sounds of Blackness. After Colorado, I was scheduled to record at Electric Lady Studios in New York for the project, where singer Brandy would cover "Optimistic" and where Karriem had asked me to put down a verse toward the end of the track. The inside of the Suburban suddenly filled up with music, the instrumental to our new "Optimistic," which included a chant: *Eyes on the prize . . . Eyes on the prize . . . Eyes on the prize.*

I asked the driver his name and I said nice to meet you. He turned to me at a red traffic light and handed me a bag. Inside the bag were three bottles of fresh-pressed juices, the kind that only exist in Los Angeles, infused with things that refortify your mind and body. My body was exhausted and sore from the workout, and I was scheduled to perform in Colorado later that night, so I accepted the juices without hesitation, taking the one I like the most for myself. I saved the other two juices for my assistant, who had on her hood and was passed out asleep with her head against the door.

As we continued to the 405, I started to rap over the instrumental. I more or less had the verse down pat, but I kept tripping over this one sequence of syllables that, when I rapped them together in succession, seemed to put me just a second or two behind the beat, so then when I moved on to the next verse, I couldn't keep the timing, and I had to start over. I wanted to get this right before heading to the studio to lay it down, and certainly before the listening session.

Karriem, Robert, and I wanted fresh ideas for the collaboration with respect to visuals, presentation on the stage, anything that would further boost the music and make it an overall entertaining experience, so I decided to schedule a listening session with some key people whose opinions I trust. The listening session was slated to occur in Los Angeles a day after I got back from Colorado, then soon after that I'd go to New York to continue recording and tweaking the album. I had to practice, with the hopes of re-recording my vocals in LA in time for the listening session, making the verse good enough to then record for the final time in New York.

I could've just as easily skipped the song during the listening session, but if I could get some feedback from live listeners, and if I had the opportunity to see for myself some initial response to the music, in whole, then it was up to me to make it happen, even if that meant extra work in the studio, or perhaps annoying everyone in the Suburban with my loud music, rapping my verse aloud over the instrumental. The traffic was, by the grace of God, clear on the 405 as the driver sped down the middle lane to the airport.

When we arrived, our greeter met us at the curb, ready with our boarding passes, to usher us through security PreCheck.

After security, the greeter escorted us to one of those carts with the yellow lights; he got behind the wheel and whipped us through the terminal with sharp turns and surprising speed. We got to the gate with a few minutes to spare, so I jogged to a newsstand we had passed to buy a couple of magazines for the flight. When I was paying for them, someone tapped me on the shoulder, and I turned to see a blond woman with two small children, a boy and a girl, and she said she was a fan and she saw me on the Oscars and she didn't want to bother me and she hoped she wasn't bothering me and she apologized for bothering me, but—she wanted to know if I would take a selfie with her and her kids. I said yes, of course—Common doesn't mind taking selfies, even though Rashid was preoccupied with thoughts of his daughter, and in these situations I make my choice to love. We took the pictures and wished each other safe travels.

The flight was preparing to board by the time I returned to

the gate with my magazines, stopped for three more photo re-
quests along the way—one guy said I kicked Keanu's butt in *John
Wick: Chapter 2* and I laughed—and the greeter was able to get
us on board early, after the parents with infants, the disabled,
and military personnel. I shook our greeter's hand—Julio was
his name—and peeped the little gold bracelet on his wrist, which
looked fresh, and I'm not even sure why it caught my attention.

The plane landed smoothly in Denver ten minutes ahead
of time. Alexandra met us at the gate and escorted us through
the airport; she had been our greeter the last time we flew in
and out of Denver. I asked her about her sister, and Alexandra, in a long black skirt and jacket, said she was fine, doing
well, and I asked her if she was on the list for the show, and
Aun said yes, everything's taken care of; Alexandra thanked
us. We descended on escalators. Below, we waited for a train
to take us from our terminal to the baggage claim, and when
we had gotten on, ridden for a minute, then gotten off and
out of the complex, another truck waited for us with its doors
opened. We climbed in; Alexandra closed my door behind me
and through the half-rolled window thanked me again for the
tickets; I thanked her for getting us out of the airport in one
piece, and she smiled and waved as the truck pulled off.

I leaned forward and asked the driver for the AUX cord,
and she said she didn't have one. *Strange*, I thought. "It's Blue-
tooth," she said, pointing at the stereo dash.

"It's okay," I said. "How far to the hotel?"

"About thirty minutes," she replied, then maybe another thirty minutes from the hotel to the venue; a printout of my itinerary was on the front passenger seat.

I couldn't change the fact that the car ride to our hotel in downtown Denver would take thirty minutes; I've come to accept these moments as my downtime, increasingly so, and the blocks are small. I cram within them as much as I can before I have to move again. And even when I have the time, say thirty minutes on the interstate into Denver, surrounded by flat land and distant Rockies, I'm distracted by the next reminder of an upcoming event, a thing I must do.

"We're not going to have time to chill," I heard Aun saying as she scrolled through her phone to reconfirm any changes while we were in flight. "We'll barely have time for dinner before the show if you want to sit down, but then I should probably look for a place now, and still you'll have, at most, ninety minutes to eat, but that's if we check in and drop our bags in the rooms and bounce all in, like, five minutes."

"Okay," I said as she looked down at her iPhone for nearby restaurants.

"There's a place across the street from the hotel with good reviews, which is perfect," she said.

"Make a reservation," I said to Aun, "please."

In thinking about my daughter, I could sense how on edge

my nerves felt. I told myself it was okay to feel worried, that I should feel worried for my daughter when she tells me I've let her down, and I should perhaps sit with the worry and, for now, do nothing else.

She and I would speak again; there would be a time for us to resume our conversation, and speaking of time, and making use of it, this was not it, at present. I hoped she called, but I didn't want to reach out just yet, not because I couldn't deal but because I wanted to have something real to say to her, true words. And if she didn't call me?

That could mean anything, too, and I shouldn't read too much into it; but then it would be up to me to reach out; and on and on it goes, parents and their adult children, I'm now learning, circling each other, waiting each other out, wondering who'll call first, who will first say *It's been long enough* . . . Meanwhile, I felt as though I understood my daughter; I was hopeful of what would happen next; my body relaxed; I started writing on my phone, thinking about my father, as a white bird stretched its wings in flight as though it transformed into a puff of white cloud that blended with the blue sky, soaring somewhere over Denver.

PART THREE

I have decided to stick with love. Hate is too great a burden to bear.

—Dr. Martin Luther King Jr.

————

'm moved when I think about love, and about purpose. I feel vulnerable, putting myself on the line, to expose my need to love and be loved. But no one said it would be easy, certainly not my mother, whose love in my life is the greatest on Earth—her love was not easy, and it came with some difficulty, I now know.

Sometimes, the world appears so dark; the world is constantly at war now. This world is one of violence and survival, but it's also one of redemption and hope. God is alive, and there is more to the world than what we see and feel now, here and now, as He offers all hopes to each of us, to be pursued until the end. We live in a world where glimmers of love peek through, revealing cracks of light behind the scenes.

It's normal, maybe, to take from love only what you desire and to leave the rest behind, to leave the work, the practice.

I did the same thing before. I know that love can heal, and I know love can build and create, but why does it hurt so much? What is the problem?

We each have a role to play in our shaping of the world. I am an artist, and a lover. I live in love; I speak in love; I move with love in mind; I act with love as my guide; I pray to God because I love; I love the world because I love; it is that simple. And to love—if the word has any meaning left, if it is to stand for anything worthwhile—means not to stand in opposition, but to stand *with*, and to live *within*. I don't want to watch the world from a distance. I'd rather open up and live the best way I can, with my hopes, with daily practice and hard work, with real effort. I want to live in a hopeful world.

Turning to God requires one to turn over one's doubts, to hand them over, to trust in each and every decision made. There is no need to fear when trusting God, but everything I know about love comes back to being vulnerable, exposed, to just—be and say whatever is necessary, so long as I am honest, and the words I say are true to me. Everything else is outside of my control. The good thing, though, is that love is a practice. But no one said it would be easy to love another person, whether a daughter or a spouse, a mother or a best friend.

Though each of us is at the center of our life, our world, we still live with one another. We're dependent on one another, whether we admit it or not. We rely on one another. And without the day-to-day practice of loving other people, and ourselves, love itself remains just an idea. In love, all things are possible. With God, there is nothing we cannot overcome. But deep and serious reflection is required; now I understand why few people bother diving so deeply into love. It's painful. It's terrifying. The deeper you go, the more you learn about yourself, and the deeper you dig, the wider the hole, the more love you can contain within; it's not easy work.

An unexamined life is not worth living.

—Socrates

———

I've been seeing a therapist since 2012, when I was really going through some things in my life. I mentioned something about how I was feeling to my acting coach, who said, "I know this therapist who can help you talk about everything." Her name is Susan. When I first spoke to her, I was in my Brooklyn apartment, sitting on my bed. I called her and introduced myself, then said plainly, "I need to talk to you." And during that first call, after I explained to her everything that was going on, I asked her some questions about why I felt the way I did. I don't recall having any negative feelings about speaking to a therapist; I figured the best thing for me was to enter into the conversation with an open mind. Besides, it was for my benefit; I wanted an outside, objective opinion on me, which, in my mind, would help me check in on myself. After that first call, we had regular sessions over the phone; at the time, I was always on the move and too busy to visit an office every week.

She made herself accessible, and I gradually felt more and more comfortable speaking with her. And since then, Susan has helped me get to the root of my issues. One thing we've unpacked and found out is something she calls "intimacy avoidance."

Because I *do* avoid intimacy at times. I found out, in talking with Susan, that this originates and still lingers from my childhood. We talked about my being raised by a single mother and how, in a situation like that, my mother, unbeknownst to her, sometimes placed some responsibility on me when I was young, especially after my father left. As a child, you can't take on all of that. But you try to, of course, because you love your mother and you want nothing but the best for her. True, sometimes it felt overwhelming for me as a child, even though I probably didn't express it, or know how to recognize the load on my shoulders. It's natural, I think, for a human to put on their child all the love they have to give. The love is great, but sometimes, at least for me, it felt like responsibilities were placed on me that I could never fulfill.

When it comes to relationships, this means that when I start feeling like I'm being pulled too much toward another person, when it feels like I'm needed too much for comfort, I tend to run away. It doesn't feel good to me; inside, something awakens, an old feeling that makes me say, *No, I don't want to take on all of your stuff.* Granted, as an artist, I need freedom and independence; I need space. Being an artist, my creative schedule is not normal when compared to someone with a steady nine-to-five job or some professional career. For me, it's all about finding that space, that feeling, where I have my freedom. When I'm in a relationship, this independence is necessary for me, and I recognize the importance of communicating this need, all while making sure my partner is okay, too. Striking this balance, this harmony, remains for me a struggle.

I remember having a conversation with a friend of mine, an actress and fellow artist, about this very point. We talked about relationships and how, sometimes, your partner has to understand that when you're going to film a movie, you might not be accessible, or as accessible as before. You may talk to them at some point, but for those months you're filming, you're engulfed in that work; you're focused on the role in front of you, the script, the mindset of the character you're looking to portray. Maybe we'll see each other on the weekends, at best, if possible. But that's what it takes to work in film, and it takes a lot to have a person in your life understand that. This is the space that we have to love the art we do, and to put that energy into the art, that passion.

This has been, I admit, a constant battle for me, to say nothing of all the other issues I've been acknowledging and actively working to improve. I know it's important that I make sure I put the same amount of love and passion that I put into music and acting into my relationship, too, every day, making the choice to be present, active, and attentive. For me, it's learning how to distribute that love and passion and to communicate effectively. There's an ebb and flow. When I need that space to work, to just *be*, hopefully my partner will understand and not take it personally. And when there is time for us to spend with each other, I can enjoy it and have a good time. But when I say I want "space," I think at times I'm hiding within that word the fear or avoidance of intimacy, the fear of being responsible for someone else's emotions. And in true love, that's not exactly what it's about, even though I'm there to support, nurture, care for, and be compassionate toward my partner's emotional needs. I should know I can't take on the responsibility for anybody else's emotions, that even someone trying to place that burden on me should be a red flag. I know I can't (and shouldn't) carry the weight, their baggage; I can give them as much as possible to try to help them through. But first, there is the fear, that irrational and powerful fear, real and ever-present.

. . .

Recently, my mother and I were both in Manhattan together; we participated in an event at a school, "Adopt a Classroom."

My mother is an educator, and we had attended this kind of event together before. This time, she stayed with me in Brooklyn. It was great to have her around, that we could be together to spend some time; we don't get a lot of time alone these days. Usually, I'm just in town for a short period, a day or two, unless it's the holidays and I fly down to Florida for an extended stay. Anyway, while in Brooklyn, she stayed at my apartment and I had to leave the city for work. The plan was that while I was out of town, she was supposed to check into a hotel. I was returning to New York for a show, and she planned to attend, so I figured I would pick her up at the hotel and then ride over to the venue. But she said, "I'm going to stay here at the apartment while you're gone." And I replied, "No, just go to your hotel and I'll pick you up from there." She was hurt and upset by the way I communicated it, and probably by the push-back in general, the issue I took with her deciding on her own to stay at my place when I wasn't there. Later, at the venue, we stood under a tent before the show, away from others for privacy, and we were able to talk through it. I apologized for the way I had communicated, but not for wanting my space. Communication always seems easier to me in my mind; in practice, in the moment, it can feel like I'm choosing the wrong word, or expressing the wrong tone, when all I'm trying to do is be open and say something clearly, and then to just listen. It's something I'm learning to do, and I feel I can grow as far as communicating in a relationship, friendship, or with my family. It's talking about the things I need, but doing so with respect and love.

Another thing I found out about with my therapist is the relationship between intimacy avoidance and the fear of abandonment, how these two things combine and influence each other to foster unhealthy thoughts and behaviors. The fear of abandonment goes back to my father not being there while I was growing up. It's strange because, in retrospect, I didn't feel abandoned by my father, and even now I am quick to correct someone if they use the word "abandonment" in relation to him. But maybe somewhere deep down inside, there was a seed planted, and eventually in a relationship, something triggered up whatever was there, waiting in silence. But fear of abandonment can show up in different ways. It's a kind of anxiety that something bad is going to happen—this person is going to do something to let me down, or show something about themselves that I can't deal with. As a result, the relationship changes and is no longer what I thought it was going to be. I realized that I haven't been able to open my heart completely, and love freely, because of these fears. I get tired of the person, of their issues, and I feel like this thing isn't going to work out, and then I have to go through the pain of hurting somebody by pulling away.

Once, I was interested in this woman although, at first, it

didn't seem to me like we would be a good fit together. That is, when I first met her, I thought she wasn't my type; but again, I wanted to keep an open mind. And as I got to know her, I saw that she had a good heart and a certain power about her; she had been through a lot, but it was obvious that in spite, or because of, it all, she maintained a warm and generous presence. My heart was open to her, and I wanted to be there and help her. But Susan said, "Well, it seems like you're attracted to those particular qualities in women because those were some of the things you saw in your mother. She was a powerful woman in your life, who was hurt by her relationship with your father. There's something about this dynamic that appeals to you; it's something that you like in a woman."

Still, even after I thought about it, I kept having this strong feeling. Some people call it "butterflies," or a tingle in the stomach, when your heart is open to another person, when it feels like it's stirring. I shared my feelings with Susan and she replied, "This is just a part of love addiction." I hadn't heard it phrased that way before; it never occurred to me that someone could be addicted to love. She explained love addiction to me, how it is related to intimacy avoidance, and how sometimes, it's more about the chase, the addiction to pursuing someone, and not about true love. That was deep for me, to be honest, to have this confident and strong, safe place where I could communicate these things to someone and finally address the wounds.

She said that feeling of butterflies, the tingle, is something I always seek out. I want that person to really put their attention on me. It's wanting that person to give me the attention, all of the love and the effort, to reciprocate the chase. When I unpack and open it up, I see now that it's not the true way to love someone; it's an addiction to being needed, an addiction to a specific physical feeling. Still, it's strange how the emotional stirring manifests itself through the physical, right in my gut. Like a certain jolt, a feeling of power. Maybe it's why I like powerful women. Not that there is anything wrong with that in and of itself. But if I need a powerful woman to give me all of this attention, all so I can feel more powerful myself, what does that say about me? Does that mean I'm not as strong and confident in myself as I like to believe? This only adds to the addiction; it's a part of the addiction. I have to work on self-love, in other words.

Which means doing things to focus on me, to focus on God, to really take the time to live within those very wounds, and to examine those wounds. To see and say for myself, *This is why I'm feeling this way.* I started declaring that I'm enough, that God's love is enough for me. I'm enough. I know who I am, and to focus on all the things that make me whole and grounded, the things that make me the reflection of God that I'm created to be, is an act of self-affirmation and self-realization. It's enough just to accept those things from a more levelheaded place, from a less needy space, and to operate on a higher level for myself, on a higher vibration. It doesn't all happen overnight or right away; it takes time to heal. But I've been able to watch my thoughts go by, and recognize how much God's love is enough for me. I remind myself of all that I am.

By having God's love, and realizing every day what God created me to be, and accepting who I am right now, and what I am working to become in the future—all of this gives me a solid stance, a foundation, and an illumination into myself. This is the beginning of the work: consistently checking in on why I'm feeling a certain away, or to see if I'm falling into old patterns again, all while building myself up, instead of tearing myself down, or running away in fear.

Later, Susan sent me an article on love and psychology. It had some questions I could ask myself. And one of the things that it really had me examine was: Have I ever just taken six months without *any* type of romance? It talked about patterns. And I realized that this has been a pattern for me, this lack of time to myself, absent any dating or relationships. Sometimes in dealing with love addiction, I create dreams and fantasies where I feel like I can heal the other person and become someone who they need. This was the trickiest part I discussed with Susan after I read the article. Naturally, I want to help people; that's my nature, to want to give love in that way. It is the savior part that comes into play when that hole within me needs to be filled, when it feels like *Oh, I need to be needed more*. It's not really like me saying, *I'm about to be the hero*. It's more like *This will make the person need me. This will make this person love me. And of course, I want to be loved*. Somehow, and somewhere along my journey in life, I learned to think that love received is just being needed.

But then, there's intimacy avoidance. Meaning, I'm addicted to something but I'm almost allergic to it as well. I need to be needed, and then once I go through that stage where the butterflies wear off, and I'm looking at the person, and I'm looking at myself, and out of all that floating and dreaming, love becomes *relationship*, something beyond feeling, something real and full of responsibility, the real and active practice of love, in other words—then I'm like, *Aw man, I don't want to be needed like that. It's too much!* It's an emotional high; I've never tried heavy drugs before, but maybe the feeling is similar to a certain degree. I still go out into the world to work and create art, but somehow that other person takes priority over so many other things in my life. When I come down from that high, reality says, *Wait! I got all these things I love to do, and now I'm in a relationship where I've created unrealistic expectations for myself and for the other person, expectations that can't be met*. Then, I'm not making as much time for the person. I pull away. Eventually I say, *Look, this isn't going to work for me, I don't want to continue in this relationship because I don't believe I want to be in a long-term commitment.* That intimacy avoidance comes in because some of my wounds start getting brushed against. And that's where I now sit down with myself and try to process things. You can't think a relationship will fill that space of self-love, of God's love, and fulfill you completely in that deeply satisfying way.

I thought it was all about the other person, but I had to be okay with my flaws and be comfortable enough to let the other person see those flaws without running away. And that's easier said than done. You go through this cycle of sorts, and you repeat old habits and scripts, things that you feel like you can't even help doing. You repeat the habits that you know you have to break, or at least understand. At some point, I think we all ask ourselves: *Why do I keep making these same decisions that I know play out exactly the same way? I can't help myself. Why can't I help myself when I'm doing these things? Why do I feel trapped?* If you're like me, you're in these moments of highs, so you throw yourself into these relationships without some reflection on what's truly good for you at that moment in time. And what do you really get from these situations? Because maybe that's the other side of it— maybe you're not getting what you really need. When I throw myself into those situations, I get the feeling that I'm important, that I'm needed by somebody who I admire and somebody who I'm learning to care about, someone I'm inspired by. And now—I can't fail them. I don't want to fail anybody. When Omoye called and talked to me that day, I felt like I'd let her down. And when my mother is going through a lot, and I can't deliver what she needs, I feel like I've let her down. It's one more fear of mine when it comes to relationships. *Am I going to let this person down? Can I deliver?* What I'm learning through therapy now is—maybe I'm asking myself the wrong questions.

• • •

All of this starts with my relationship with my mother, because it's from her that I first learned love, a healthy and strong love that has guided and stuck with me throughout life; it's not her fault that I'm now dealing with love addiction and intimacy avoidance, and my work with a therapist isn't about assigning blame on her, or absolving myself of any decisions I've made as an adult. But through therapy, I am learning a lot more about patterns, how things repeat themselves not just in our personal lives, but generationally, from ancestor to descendant, mother to son, and father to daughter. As a child, my mother wasn't raised around her father, just like I wasn't, and to some extent, just like Omoye, my mother has had her own feelings of abandonment, to say nothing of when she and my father split up. These are things that I wouldn't have known had I not talked to a therapist, and even my mother is now just discovering some of this for herself as she continues her own work.

The feeling of falling in love is something powerful. Though now I ask myself, *But do I really need that feeling to be in a healthy relationship, and what does it mean if that feeling fades, or changes?* Maybe it's not always necessary to feel that high, but I know I want to feel it—maybe that's the addiction talking. I'm a passionate person by nature; it's the energy I draw from to do all the work that matters most to me. Anything I do from a place of love must have passion in it. Otherwise, why else do it when there are so many things in life that could potentially inspire and amplify passion? In a potential relationship, I want the other person to have that same intense level of passion for whatever it is that they do in their lives, personally, professionally, and artistically. I hope they have a passion for changing the world, for being a positive light, not just for me as their potential partner, but for all people, as many people as possible.

I think, throughout my life, I've had pockets where I've wanted the other person to elevate me, or felt as though they were going to provide a kind of boost for me to approach my higher self. I think, *Why wouldn't love elevate me?* But it's not fair to my partner to assign such responsibility to them; to a degree, a relationship should always elevate both people involved; you want to feel as though there is some obvious, tangible improvement to your emotional well-being from actively building a relationship with this partner. But a higher self? That's God's work. God is the one who can fill me up, who gives me my full light and full power. Because God is in me, and love develops the God within me. It's why I revisit the New Testament; I'm often inspired by the life of Jesus the way someone might be inspired to solve a puzzle, a mystery. His heart was open to every man, and in every man he saw the capacity for forgiveness because, as far as I can tell in my reading, he saw in every man himself. Not from an egotistic point of view, but from a human perspective, the truth that while each of us is different and has unique capabilities, we are each one of us the same, fundamentally.

We all dream; we all suffer; we all try to make sense of our pains in the quest for healing; and we all make mistakes, are perfect in our imperfection. And if I dare to see all of this in myself—if I seek God in me through a higher self—that means I have to dare to see myself in other people, to see God in everyone. This is active work, I realize; I have to extend myself past contemplation and reading, beyond writing rhymes and reciting them in the recording booth, or performing songs onstage. There's more I can do, more I should do, in the name of love. Someone I'm in a partnership with isn't going to be the defining moment or source of my power, of my greatness as a human being, nor will they point me to my purpose. That partner can only support me as I walk the path I'm already on, and sharpen my perspective so I can see the light in them and in myself, and hopefully, in every person.

When I wake up in the morning, I thank God for the day; I claim my day. And again, I turn to the New Testament to read my favorite scriptures. When I re-read them, I always think, *How can I apply these words within my everyday life? These stories, these wise words that are being told generation to generation, how can they become gems for me to walk with in my everyday life? How can I practice? What should I do? How can I overcome some of the things that are going on in this world, and the things that I'm going to encounter throughout this one day?* With prayer, and by reading the Bible, the Koran, other religious texts and new books, and with meditation, I establish a daily and consistent practice for myself. As I go along, some things will be changed or enhanced; I'll add to the practice, but the important thing is to continue practicing this relationship with myself, and with God.

And when you practice, you start to recognize that God is in all these beautiful places and people, and in the struggle. It's a real relationship you have to build, something that goes beyond religious ideas. It's an intimate relationship, personal and ever evolving. And it is one that has helped me to forgive a lot of the things that have happened in the past, things I may have been a part of. It helps me to recognize and claim my cosmic light. Through therapy, through practice, I want to arrive at a place of forgiveness. Forgiveness can remove whatever separates you from someone else. It reminds me of the real, actual power we have, no matter who may tell us otherwise. You have power; you are worthy; within you is a real light; the question is how? How can we get out of the way and let our light shine through? How can we see it in ourselves?

. . .

Presence of mind is something I've had to work on over time, and it has been one of the greatest lessons of my life. I have this habit, and maybe it's something you can relate to, where I often dwell on past moments and feelings, long after actual events have occurred. I spend so much time worrying about how this thing happened—something, mind you, I can't change since it's happened and now in the past—or how I behaved in some moment a long time ago. It feels like I can never really move on or be serious about what's happening right now, to say nothing about planning with a clear mind for the future, thinking through the next moves, the next steps so I am always heading in the right direction. But when I started working on being present, on making that kind of effort for myself and for those I love, life began to feel more vibrant, alive. It's a matter of saying simply, *I'm here, man—just enjoying this one life of mine, looking to experience all that I can here and now.*

Before I was going on stage at the Academy Awards to perform "Glory," one of the producers of *Selma* was like, "Yo, don't choke up on me. It's gonna be a billion people watching!" I said, "I guess you trying to make us nervous." To be honest I wasn't nervous as much as I was excited. I said to myself, *Man, I'm just going to be present for this, and just be in the moment. I can't let it pass, and I can't worry or be concerned about nervousness or anything like that. Just focus on my purpose and be present. That's it.*

I saw Bradley Cooper afterward, and he said, "You just seemed really present when you were doing that performance." And I said, "Man, that's the perfect word for it: *present.*" It felt amazing to be there, to feel as though I was one with everything and everyone around me. That was a spiritual moment of being present. It has become a consistent practice and work, but it's so fulfilling and life-affirming. It's empowering. I'm not sitting there worrying about something that happened three days ago, and I'm not stressing out about three days from now, like *This is going to be crazy.* I kind of allow "three days from now" to handle itself; no one knows what will happen in the next instant, but there is a trust, a feeling—love, I think—that becomes evident the more present you are in the moment.

I put my trust in God, and remind myself, *I can only do these things right now.* Presence of mind goes to the heart of becoming an active participant in love. It's difficult to love someone—impossible, maybe—if you're not present.

One of the greatest gifts you got is presence of mind, and when it comes to love there is nothing more pure and divine you can provide. Because if you work on consistently allowing yourself to be here, in the present, you'll naturally let go of so much of the drama and negativity; you won't hold on to things that happen, or hold things against someone for what they've done, especially when someone has made a mistake. You become more forgiving without really trying or thinking about it. When you're present, you understand that that was something that happened in the past; nothing you can do about it now, and no amount of grasping onto the negative energy will change what happened.

But you don't have to put that person's past onto them, like extra weight placed on their shoulders. (As if they don't have enough to carry; as if we all don't.) Presence of mind gives you the power to choose how *you* will react and behave in a situation. Besides, if the person has made a choice and declared to you that they want to do better, and you see them actively working to change their behavior, then there's not much else for you to do, other than mind your own feelings and watch your own reactions. The issues I've had with relationships come from the past, not the present. If I could really just love in the present, I could love in the greatest way possible for all of us—in a whole and complete way that is healthy, flexible, and beneficial.

. . .

There's a barrier or something preventing me from having that presence of mind in every situation, but I'm working toward overcoming it. The more I check in on myself, assessing and gauging where I am, the closer I get. Knowing what I want in love has allowed me to say, *Okay, this is what is most important for me.* It's about knowing those things, and some of those things can of course change with time. But the consistent things, the ones that remain with me, are a good heart, a belief in God, and a practice of being loving and compassionate toward other people. I look for opportunities to extend myself and to try to foster healing. That is love for community. That is the spirit behind activism. It is at the heart of socially active work, something that I've been inspired to do more of in the wake of Michael Brown's death in Ferguson, Missouri, which occurred while I was working on set for *Selma.*

Getting to do *Selma* helped me gain a new love and reverence for the civil rights movement, which I got to know better and more intimately while working on the movie. As time went on, I began to be even more impassioned and inflamed by what had happened. As we walked on the same path, I felt we had to continue those steps they walked during the movement, and to continue everything they were doing. The walk they began, we got to continue it. And that's when I started to feel that love. With Ava DuVernay there as the leader, and with all these different actors and people and the crew around, I felt part of a movement that was bigger than any of us. And then I got to play this character every day, someone who was one of the components of the civil rights movement and the March on Washington.

I've developed some of the best friendships I have ever had in this industry from *Selma*. From Ava, to André Holland, to Colman Domingo, to Tessa Thompson, to Omar Dorsey, and all these people; they're like family to me now. And we went through that experience together, and that means something to all of us. So that love, that was the ultimate—that was when I found out I could be a part of films that have a socially conscious purpose and not be preachy, but just—show the humanity. Because the thing that I really loved about *Selma* was it gave us more insight into Dr. King as a man, too, and the people of the movement. You saw a man who was fighting every day for the movement, but was also having outside affairs and spending time away from his children. It made me think, too, that when you're working for the people, and do for God and a higher cause, there can be people around you who suffer sometimes.

We can never use the work as an excuse to make loved ones suffer, or be like *This is a mighty deed I'm doing, so you don't get your father as much*. It's not like that, but the work is driving you so much to do these things for the world that sometimes you don't look and say, *I just need to go sit down and watch her do her homework*. That's important, too. And I always consider, I always look at myself and say, *Okay, you feel like you want to make all this change in the world and do all these things, but you have to make sure your home is in the right place and you put in that energy*. But it is a conflict in some ways. It doesn't have to be a conflict, maybe, but if you direct your energy toward bigger issues and causes, that takes a lot of effort, and you have to be aware to be able to maintain that balance in life and parenting.

Balance is the gift that if you open it up, it will serve you and you will appreciate more. Maybe, more than solving my issues or healing my wounds, what I want from love is balance. I think that's what I was trying to get across to Omoye. Like, *I hope you know, and I want you to know, that the love was always there, and the love is there right now. Because I couldn't spend some of that time with you, that doesn't mean I didn't love you. Now I understand why you felt like I might not have made the effort, and that can make you question,*

Where's my dad? *I understand that. I hear what you're saying, and I respect you. I can try to save the world, but I'm still your father, too.*

. . .

This work has widened my idea of love and its power to heal, and has brought me face-to-face with my own limitations and shown me my room for growth. There's a negative energy in certain places in the world that I feel like is the enemy. And I don't want to succumb to it. When I'm face-to-face with that enemy, that negative energy, I look to see if there's a way for me to not be at my worst, and to always see the human being in every situation.

In 2017, I visited four state prisons in California: Calipatria, Lancaster, Ironwood, and the California Institution for Women. My intention was to go and talk to the men and women incarcerated, but mainly just to sit and listen, to hear their stories. I visited the prisons with Scott Budnick and his organization called ARC, or the Anti-Recidivism Coalition. While there, I met some of the most enlightened human beings, who were also serving life without parole for various crimes. It was a life-enhancing and sobering experience for me. I was set to perform at these prisons, which was a first for me—I wasn't quite sure what to expect and it was a little difficult to imagine. The stage was erected in each of the yards, and I remember watching the setup and thinking how amazing it was that I could have the opportunity to perform my music in such a setting as a maximum security prison; I hoped I was bringing a little light to the residents; I wanted to do my best for them.

I remember the visit to Lancaster, where it was so windy outside that we couldn't set up the stage, so unfortunately, I was unable to perform. But I was there with some city and state legislators and administrators, so while we were disappointed that I couldn't perform, the opportunity was there for us to think about and talk through actual policy change, based on real, face-to-face conversations with the prisoners. Scott said, "Let's just set up a circle and talk to some brothers who are locked up here without parole." And we sat with the warden, the governor's chief of staff, and others, along with the prisoners, all in a circle. And we just talked about different things, had opportunities to ask questions and to listen. It was incredible.

We went around the circle introducing ourselves, and each inmate would say their name, like, "I'm Mike, and I killed John Wilson and Derek Jones." They each would say the names of the people who they killed. They'd say, "I'm serving time and I murdered . . ." I asked, "Why do you say the people's names?" The whole experience was new to me, and I didn't want to make any assumptions for them; I wanted to hear what they had to say. And one inmate replied, "Man, we want to humanize them; we should humanize them. And I recognize that at the time, when I did that, I didn't look at him like a human being. That man, on the other side of the thing I did, the crime I committed, I didn't even look at him as human. I want his family to know I look at him as a human being. I want to humanize him for myself, so that I feel more humanity in me."

And the men in the circle shared how much regret they carried—so many of them were saying how much they regret doing those things and they can't get those moments back. But they just want to be human beings now, and to live and be treated as such, whether in prison for life or not. I remember this one dude, Carlos, who spoke up and said, "Imagine if you were seventeen years old. Imagine you did something at age seventeen and you been trapped in here for that act for the rest of your life. Think of the places you wouldn't have been able to go: the White House, to Japan and France. Think of the things you wouldn't have been able to do, just from one act." Many of the men there had been locked up since age seventeen, doing life without parole; they called it "L-WOP." Don't get me wrong—some of these brothers took people's lives, and they recognized the weight of what they'd done, but at a certain point, it has to be some type of healing and forgiveness, and shutting down the senseless cycle. We said a prayer at the end and I felt God in that moment. Because it didn't matter whether you were the warden or the governor's chief of staff or somebody who had murdered two individuals and was doing life without parole—we were all human beings. There was no judgment, no comment, it was just like—*we're all in here*.

Later, we were interviewing different people, and I had an opportunity to visit the cells. Tamara, who works alongside me, visited the prisons with us, and she was talking to this one dude. She was saying bye through the cell, and his cellmate came up and said bye, too, using this hand signal with the pinkie finger that they would do through the cell bars. Tamara looked back and she saw this Green Bay Packers stuff on the walls, and she asked, "You like the Packers?"

He was like, "Yeah, but I shouldn't, though. I'm from Chicago."

Tamara said, "What? You're from Chicago?" Like me, Tamara is from Chicago, too. We ended up talking to Robert, who, like some of the other people we spoke to, had left the gang life behind while in prison. So he was talking about this transition and his family, and we ended up wanting to talk to some of his family members, too. Robert mentioned his sister, who was really his cousin but who he considered his sister since she was the closest person to him, and how he hadn't seen her in seventeen years; he went in sometime around 2000. He hadn't seen her, and his son, so maybe we could talk to his son, too. I don't think his son wanted to talk, but we did end up talking to his sister, his cousin, about three days after we'd seen Robert.

We met at her house, and I was talking to her about what it's like missing her cousin, her family member, someone who's incarcerated. All the while, we were being filmed for a future documentary. And the director said to her, "Tell him the story." I was like, *What is she about to say?*

She went into the story of the day that the murder happened, the one Robert was eventually convicted of, and she said, "I drove him to where we were, to this dead-end street, where this dude was lifting weights, and we got out the car . . . ," and she said, "You know, the incident happened . . . and then we got back in the car, and 'The Light' was playing. You know the song 'The Light'?"

My song "The Light" was playing in the car moments after this awful thing happened, and she said, "I turned it down, and from that point on I can never listen to that song no more." I was always a part of their story whenever she told it. And she said her family knew not to play that song, because it would take her back. And she was afraid to tell me the story. She was tearing up, and I was tearing up, because she was saying to me, "I don't know what God's saying now, now you're here in front of me, at this point. After this whole time you've been a part of that story, and now you're here at this point of my life, and this point of his life." And like, in a flash, the song was there, and it struck me, and she showed me a picture Robert had drawn, and the words underneath were poetic, and beautiful, and the last words said, "I'll forever be by your side." Those are like the words from "The Light"—"I will be by your side."

My most recent visit to a prison was to San Quentin, my first time at the facility. I can definitely say, despite my previous visits to the other prisons, San Quentin was a whole new experience. San Quentin is known as one of the more "progressive" prisons in America; a lot of their programs are adopted by other prisons throughout the country. I'm not sure what I expected from the visit; maybe I was influenced by the idea of "San Quentin," having heard the prison name so often in my adult life, especially since relocating to California. But like all situations, I wanted to approach it with an open mind or, at the very least, to draw on some important information from my previous experiences. I didn't want to arrive with too many assumptions, but I knew incarcerated people to be enlightened and empathetic human beings, independent (or perhaps because of) whatever crimes they may have committed.

When we got to the facility, one of the first things I noticed was all of the people walking around the yards. The energy there felt more unsettled to me—that's the word that came to my mind—than at some of the other prisons we had visited. I met a brother there, this musician who had come over to the

States from Sweden to work as a producer, but who got into an altercation where one man lost his life. And so, we were there in the cell, listening to the brother's music, the man from Sweden, and he said, "We wanted to do this project that connects people who are incarcerated with artists and producers who are, you know, free, or I should say, 'a part of society,' not incarcerated, in other words. We want to connect this thing so the voices of the people who are locked up in prisons can be heard, and they can therefore be humanized." That was part of our mission when we visited San Quentin and the other prisons. Later, we were walking through the cell blocks, and I had an opportunity to enter an empty cell. I went and looked at, then walked into, the cell. It felt claustrophobic to me. If I had reached both of my own arms out, I could've probably touched wall-to-wall with my hands.

Eventually, we visited death row. In all honesty, that was the darkest place I had gone to in my life. I remember noting the building as we approached, which was made with old brick stones. San Quentin has been open since 1852, so the building looked like it had been there since then. Above the entrance, it said "Condemned Row." The guards all looked a little relaxed to me, or maybe bored, like they were used to the whole situation. But inside, there were people who did not get to see or have contact with other humans beyond the guards, and the only time they could leave their cells was for one hour per day. We walked past some of the people who were out during that hour; they were sitting on buckets in the middle of what appeared to me to be a cage. One of the guys on death row had kidnapped and killed a young girl. There was another inmate who had killed twelve people. The sorrow, the despair, was unimaginable to me. The whole building had its own smell, and it was figuratively and literally darker than the other parts of the prison. Some of the other places I've visited within the prison system, like some of the yards, for example, had hope. I could feel it, and I could see a glimmer of light, a little flicker that was coming through in the way the men and women spoke and interacted with one another. But death row felt hopeless to me, heavier and somber. One of the men hollered, "Is that Common?" He said to me, "Common, I like what you doing. But make sure you give back. Make sure you give back to the community. Yeah, go get your money. Go do it, Common, that's right. But make sure you give back." It stuck with me for some reason when he said that, maybe because he addressed me personally; nevertheless, the whole time I spent during my visit to death row, I could feel the dark, hopeless energy throughout my being.

And I remember thinking, *How can I reach these men on a human level? How can I find a place to connect with them, to show love? How can I muster up love for someone who has killed a child?* Reflecting back, I can't now say that at the time I was in my deepest place of love, or even knew how to reach for it, not with the heaviness, the negativity at that moment. But once that inmate yelled my name and spoke to me, I felt like I had to find that place within myself to be loving in that moment. When he spoke, I just listened to him, and everything felt sensitive, like I was on edge, like how sometimes everything in your body feels raw, like the hairs on your skin are standing up, because you're in such a heightened, emotionally charged place. Sometimes you can be in a heightened place of joy and love, but the feeling on death row was one of darkness. I didn't want it near or to influence my own energy, but then the brother reached out and spoke to me, and I wanted to take in the moment, to humanize him, without being too guarded or aloof.

I haven't reached a level of knowing forgiveness, the kind that Jesus speaks about in the New Testament, forgiving not just seven times, but seventy-seven times. I don't think I've even been tested at that level in life yet, to be able to say, *Yeah, man, I can forgive the person who killed twelve people*. Maybe I was asking too much of myself; maybe wanting to see the humanity in these people was the best I could really do. Regardless, I had to look and understand. It's a different thing for someone who has lost a loved one to find forgiveness for the person who killed their loved one. In some respects, it's beyond my understanding; that's a real level of forgiveness, of empathy, of love, but it is also the only way I see all of us moving forward, if we all can find that place within and bring it out at all times.

What I felt in San Quentin, and certainly what I felt in death row, was that I realized I still didn't know how to truly express love in that place; I didn't know if they could really feel the love, and my humanity; I don't know, in retrospect, if I could feel their humanity. I like to think it was enough that I was there, and maybe that's not for me to say or to judge. But I do know that of all the things a person can do, no matter how much money you have, or fame or influence or so-called "power," one of the most valuable is to be present and to listen, to show up. How can anything even begin to change if you don't show up? Showing up might not feel like it's enough, but sometimes it's all you can do, and it's on you to recognize that being there is enough; it is truly enough. Still, when I walked out of that place, I said a prayer and tried to shake off all of that energy. But before I left, another one of the incarcerated men said, just as I was about to go, "Common, anytime you think things is not going right, things is messed up, think about us, man. Think about us."

• • •

I believe that those of us who practice love on a daily basis have to try to understand those people who are pushed down by society, those who are locked up in prison, and those who are largely forgotten; we have to understand them, and we have to extend our hands out to them. Practicing love in the world, from a social and communal perspective, means having to take the time to say, *I have to go beyond just the things and the people that directly affect me, beyond my everyday orbit, and beyond my own community, to also consider and think about those of us who have been forgotten in prison, who are dehumanized every day, and everyone in society who is kept down all while I'm here standing up. There's more I can do.*

Because in my mind, every soul deserves redemption. Every person deserves the chance to be forgiven, if possible, and a chance to heal themselves and, if they can, to correct the things they've experienced in their lives, to undo the damage they caused. Because love is taking time to try to understand why a person may have experienced something, knowing that you may not see things from that perspective; it's taking time to realize that, despite what the person has done, and where they are now, they deserve to be heard, cared for, nurtured, and provided the tools toward redemption and healing.

It's easy to do something for somebody who can, in return, provide something of value to you. But to just go and take some time to listen and consider those who may not have anything to do with your everyday life, who may not have anything to give you, is one way how love becomes an action word. I rap about prisons in my music, and I have the desire to help people stop mass incarceration, but what's my action? How can I show love? Well, I decided to show up. There has to be a bridge, something that leads one to listening and thinking about people, and to taking action. Having an action item to do something, to be a part of real change—that's actual love, and it can spread throughout the world.

The bridge is a symbol of sorts, a representation of this greater idea of love with respect to humanity. How to cross the bridge between oneself and the world is the question. Love is that bridge, whether that means charity work or even just being what people used to call a "good Samaritan." Even small actions can be considered love! Overall, I think we have to make the effort and reach into a deeper place of love if we want society and people to improve for all of us. If we want the world to be a better place, if we're looking for a way to manifest the best world we can imagine in our minds, we have to go to that place where it's uncomfortable for us, somewhere that we might not be used to, to perhaps do something that we, maybe at one point in our lives, didn't even think about attempting, maybe out of fear.

Yes, taking a life is a terrible thing to do; its impact rever-berates across families, countries, and generations. But love says, *I know you've done that, but I still believe and can see that you are a human being and a reflection of God. I might have made the same mistake in life, if I were in your same circumstance, and what if I was also condemned forever for that one mistake? I would want someone to see me still as a human. What if I had to go through the trauma of childhood abuse, or had a parent who was dealing with drugs and couldn't shake their addiction—what if I had to grow up with all of that? What kind of human being would I have turned out to be?*

You have to use your own humanity to find it in other people; there is no other way, and you can't see it in others until you find it in yourself. Granted, not all of us are willing or are able to visit a prison; I understand that and know it's hard enough as it is to get by on the daily. But where can you start? Some of the smallest actions are true and genuine gestures of love. One step can potentially change the world. One step is the step that might change everything. Opening the door, and holding the door, for another human being, whether for a man or a woman, for example. Seems like nothing; it seems inconsequential to world affairs, but if it's nothing then why not do it? It's beyond chivalry or good manners; you're giving that other person something that they deserve, that *you* deserve: a moment to feel cared for and valued, a moment to be seen and acknowledged, all without worrying about whether or not they say thank you.

These are just the little things we can all do to set aside our egos, if only a tiny bit. You have to be aware of when you are doing things that are not coming from a place of love; it requires presence of mind to practice. It's almost like setting up a mirror directly in front of your emotions, particularly during those times when you're feeling like you want to say something that may not be helpful toward another person. Or maybe you feel helpful but only toward what you yourself want and can get out of the situation. The point is to make sure that your actions and your words have the right intentions behind them; to maintain the possibility and capacity to uplift, shift, and empower people, yourself included, to head in a better, positive direction.

The bridge is always available, open to everyone, and this is the way certain people I respect and revere would behave, those people I view as "love giants." A love giant can be someone like Oprah, or Dr. King, or a teacher—it doesn't really matter who they are or what they do for a living. But they represent for us the kind of people we can be every day, by thinking what we can do, first by being aware of how we act toward one another, and at certain points, going out of our way to ensure that we extend compassion and understanding to the next person. It takes effort, but sometimes it's all we have, and it's all we can do.

All that we have in the world takes shape through human

effort, including ourselves. That effort is there for us to make in the smallest of situations, or in the darkest—it starts right there, in the moment that calls us to action. People need to take that thing they feel inside themselves and transform it into purposeful action in service of other people's lives. For me, I think one of the reasons why I haven't been able to be complete and full in a relationship is because, at times, I haven't been able to say, *Okay, I'm going to give this person something that will help them, and I'm not going to benefit from it, but that's okay. I should do it anyway.* By doing good toward someone else, it's helping the greater situation, something bigger than me. Everything is not going to be to my direct benefit.

But that's the beauty of it! Once you do it for the right reason, you'll see it does, in its own way, benefit you. You're doing it for love, from a place of love, and something inside of you feels confirmed, rewarded. I think because you're not doing it with the expectation of reciprocation in mind, it makes the reward sweeter. It's paradoxical to a point, but there's something about going into a situation with the intention *I'm not going to do this for my glory, or for people to recognize me for my good deeds.* The exchange is intimate, personal—it's an action that fills your heart and your soul. You give love to yourself, because love is, by its very nature, a reciprocated thing. It comes back to you. The feelings and actions you show toward another human being only go to show the connectedness we have; they reaffirm the divine way. But you have to choose love.

· · ·

I'm sure there is someone reading this and saying to themselves, *Yeah, okay, Common. I feel you about all of this, and maybe you're right. But I'm looking around. And I see people who are doing for themselves, just for themselves and with no regard for other people. They're putting out evil and negativity. They seem to be getting over. They get money, they get whatever they want, and the people out here who are trying to do good, and live in love, well they're not being heard. They're being harassed by police. They live in poverty. They can't catch a break, and it doesn't seem like there's a lot of love in their lives.*

All I can do here is share my perspective, and this is what I would say in response to this individual who, of course, isn't wrong. There are places in the world that are not receiving the love that they should, and there are governments that behave as though they do not serve and benefit the people, all of them. That said, I guarantee you that when you go into those corners of the world, and find some love in those places, because it exists anywhere, everywhere, whether in a war zone or at the site of a natural disaster, you can actually feel the difference in the face of those people engaged in love. Whether it's the Lancaster prison, or Ironwood, Cuba, or 63rd and Cottage Grove, it is there and it is alive. This active, practiced love is the only way we will halt the pain and ease people's strife. We have to stomp down on the cycle. We can see leaders who are not operating with love for their people. And if you do not operate in love as a leader, then there are going to be people left out, and you cannot claim yourself to be a leader *for all*. But if you do operate in love as a leader, you will have heard the people and will take into consideration everyone. Of course we're not always going to agree, but love is the thing that considers; it listens; it spends time and is patient enough to allow the other person or people to feel that they have been heard and acknowledged. That means going into places that you normally wouldn't go, but that's what leaders do. And it takes a real leader to say, *You know what, this situation is dire, and I cannot continue to do this just because I want things to be ruled my way.*

Maybe I'm idealistic, and I've certainly always been a dreamer, but so be it—I still think we are heading toward a better and more loving world, because so many people have had to deal with hate that, as a result, love has been activated. So many people talk about things that they want to do, or go out and be a part of something that's helping others. I see people who operate in love and want that kind of world, leaders who have been activated and awakened. Every day, they go and make the effort to find what can be done, and I think the result will be a better world. Everybody should be considered. All people need to be included. Now there are more images of different types of people on television and in films; there are women superheroes, Black show runners and creators of shows, diverse people producing movies and music. Black athletes are opening schools for kids. People are energized and charged to do things. So as tough as the world is, and as down as people have been, it really is bringing out the love and leadership in all of us, the best in us. So many of us want to be a benefit to the world. We ask ourselves, *What can I do to be a part of bettering the world?* This love will overcome the anger, the hatred.

PART FOUR

Love is a friendship set to music.

–Joseph Campbell

We never know exactly why some people gravitate toward us, or vice versa. Maybe we can point out physical traits that we like, or a person's personality, the way they express themselves; but in the vast and complex way a human being exists, these traits and expressions are like little glimmers of light that are valuable but cannot begin to display a person's full brilliance. And yet, this person is here before us, in the form of a parent, or a sibling, a new friend, or a potential life mate. The warm feelings, the good times, all the things we enjoy with another person, are all present, but the nature of love itself is greater than our comprehension of it. To me, that means there is always something new to learn and experience.

I like to think my communication with myself and with other people is improving, though I admit this continues to be a work in progress for me. Even so, that's okay so long as I'm more aware and therefore able to approach any given situation with an open mind and with a flexible mind, not being so rigid in my thinking and in my emotions that I can't see another person's point of view.

As I build a new relationship and partnership, there may be the same old doubts and anxieties, but with greater awareness I'm able to take inventory of these fears, and the situations or conditions that created them. I can recognize now an issue that is in reality a small deal, nothing significant, that I'm literally making bigger in the moment by feeding into it my anxiety, or my inability to clearly communicate a specific need. Usually when the anxiety or fear pops up, I would somehow blame the other person, like it's their fault I'm annoyed or feeling any kind of negativity. Now, I try to think through the situation, acknowledging it may very well be my own hang-ups—intimacy avoidance or love addiction, or something that stretches all the way back to my childhood—and by identifying the fears, I prevent them from interfering with the moment, and with the relationship.

And as far as communication goes, like I said it's a work in progress. The most important thing I keep in mind is the fact that my intention is not to hurt anyone; this allows me more freedom to communicate, and it makes clear for me the responsibility to speak in a compassionate way, to be as careful as possible with respect to the words I use. In one instance, my new partner and I discussed whether we should go to Sunday church service together or not. And I thought it particularly important to state clearly my wishes and the reasoning behind them.

I had gotten used to attending church by myself. I like having the time to myself to commune with God; that's my time to connect without having to think about another person's needs at that time. And I enjoy the community aspect of attending church service, of being among other people who are there to connect and worship. I can feel the presence of God in spiritual settings where more than one person is focused on the Creator. For now, it's important to me to keep this time for myself. The issue was making this known to my partner without carelessly creating negative energy. And even though we did not attend church together, in hindsight I don't think I communicated quite the way I wanted to, or in the best manner I had envisioned.

In any case, I spoke with my therapist about it to get some perspective. And we talked about the whole situation, and she clarified the reality that it was something I needed to ask for; it would have been a mistake on my part had I kept it to myself. And in a way, it's similar to the Martha Graham quote regarding expressions, and how it's not the artist's job to determine or judge whether the expression is good or bad, or whether or not it has any value. Sometimes I get so caught up in my concern over whether my communication, my expression, is good or bad, based largely on how the other person reacts to the expression, that I lose sight of the necessity to express myself at all.

In other words, if you're always more concerned about how someone will react to you, and if you're worried someone will react negatively, then you're less likely to say anything at all. And in such a situation, you're the one who ends up hurting the most. I better understand, it's not about being careless in the words you say, but it's about being clear, and then just letting it be. I should be able to ask for whatever I need; conversely, she should be able to ask for whatever she needs. Recognizing, speaking to, and honoring our truths is the correct path to fostering love and intimacy; that such communication is difficult only underscores the impact of this positive and open connection.

This is surrendering, which means to go forward with a vision and fight for everything that you desire and want; and when things don't happen smoothly, you understand that the bumps are part of the process and must be endured as you remain on the path toward your goal. Ultimately, what's your goal? Who are you? What are your capabilities? With all of this, and this vision, in mind, you can surrender to sometimes not receiving certain victories, or avoiding miscommunication, or hurting someone's feelings. All of this adds up to bettering yourself, bettering your soul, bettering your relationship; again, this all adds up to love.

Sooner or later, you have to find a way to let go of the worries that you might cling to in hopes that they'll lead you to some perfect version of yourself. Even though you do have a higher self, it is only approachable when you take a leap of faith, and dare to fall, and be brave enough to live your truths. We must be courageous. It doesn't matter if someone laughs at you, or it doesn't matter if someone doesn't like something you're doing, or doesn't like you at all; you just have to be not afraid. This is true in relationships, and it's true in life in general.

One of my best friends is a doctor, a man who has always been very regimented and disciplined in his life and in his work. He called me up one day and said, "Man, I just took my first acting class!" I was shocked. I had no idea he wanted to act, so I asked him questions about it. He said he wasn't interested in becoming an actor, but he did want to improve himself as a public speaker, so he figured an acting class might help. He's overcoming his fears and doubts to try something new, in part to improve himself in one specific area, but generally to expose himself to new pursuits and pathways. I can't begin to express how inspired I was by my friend, and how it goes to show that no matter where you are, or what you're doing, and no matter your age, you always have the chance to be brave.

I can't overstate how much therapy has helped open my eyes. Speaking with my therapist has a cathartic and cleansing effect. To have at least one space where I can talk things through without judgment, and where I can receive advice, affirmation, and criticism in a thoughtful and emotionally healthy way, is invaluable to me. There are some things I don't even know I feel. I know I'm feeling something, but I can't describe it so another person can understand me. All these complex feelings and confusion and unrest are hard to nail down in specific words, or to even try to trace back their origins to some distant moment in the past.

I think everyone can relate to having someone listen to you and respond with an illuminating word that lights up what was once dark and hidden within you. This is all the more crucial because we're so susceptible to believe we know and can see everything that goes on in our minds, but it's not always the case, especially as our lives become busier as we age and take on more responsibilities. Speaking with a professional therapist who is trained in and knowledgeable of human behavior, the mind and its clinical workings, and proven, evidence-based methods to aid your healing can change your life or, at the very least, provide a quiet, judgment-free space for you to breathe and process what might be a lifetime of pressures and strains on your spirit.

A therapist can help you describe feelings you cannot put into words, and then they can point you toward healing. Some people might not like the idea of paying another person to "listen to problems," but I would encourage anyone who has not spoken with a therapist to try it at least one time. On one hand, maybe it's not for you; but on the other hand, you would've made one sincere attempt to work on yourself.

All of this is to say, when it comes to romantic love and partnership, I'm taking things slower. My tendency to go all out at the beginning of a new relationship is fine, but the behavior isn't so good when dealing with my intimacy and communication issues. Now it's crucial for me to slow down and take deliberate steps toward building a real relationship.

Remember my conversation with Michelle Obama in the White House? When she told me I should compromise in finding my ideal partner? Well, I saw her again, this time on *The Late Show with Stephen Colbert*. She was a guest and I was there to perform a medley of songs inspired by the former First Lady. We had a chance to speak backstage. Mrs. Obama asked me, "Are you taking my relationship advice? You have to apply it! You have to put it into practice." Later, we were sitting on Stephen Colbert's couch, and I told her a little bit about my new relationship. Mrs. O said, "Take it slow, get to know the person," and she reminded me once again that no one is perfect. Meanwhile, Stephen Colbert finally sat down and asked us what we were talking about. Mrs. O replied, "Oh, I'm just his counselor." I laughed, and I said, "I got a great counselor here!"

Societies never know it, but the war of an artist with his society is a lover's war, and he does, at his best, what lovers do, which is to reveal the beloved to himself and, with that revelation, to make freedom real.

—James Baldwin

———

A
s I said before, there were times when I didn't see or have positive examples of partnership in my life. I couldn't draw from earlier experiences shared between loved ones to see for myself how love manifests itself between two adults who, for whatever reason, decided to spend their lives with each other, even a portion of the time, whether months or years. I was just a year old by the time my parents had broken up, and I sometimes wonder what I missed out on—not just the time, the memories, shared together as a family unit, but just as a young boy having the opportunity to see his father love his mother, and vice versa, and all that is included. Even the would-be fights and disagreements would've been a valuable experience, I think, in providing a template for how to

handle rough moments where me and my loved one can't see eye-to-eye. And the apologies—how much did I miss out on seeing real, heartfelt apologies? Not just platitudes—*I'm sorry* or *I'll never hurt you again*—but the shifts in behavior; to see for myself my father or mother changing in real time in the name of the other person's feelings. Why? To make sure that the other person is cared for, and protected, and provided the love and respect they deserve just because they exist, and they are loved.

In retrospect, it's asking too much of our parents to uphold themselves in idealistic ways; inevitably, they fall down, as we all do. But again, there's value for a child to see his parents pick themselves up, hand in hand, together, as a pair. And I look around at my friends and peers who grew up differently than I did, from different cities and with wildly different circumstances, and it's hard for me to say for sure if our lives are really universal. That is, we're all human and we all share common traits and feelings—intellectually, this is easy to understand. But it's another thing to realize it and bring out this reality with empathy and wisdom. I don't know why I am the way I am, and why I see the world the way I do, but I can point to moments in time during my formative years that made the difference, perhaps, in why I walked one path and not another.

My biological parents' relationship and their struggles had some role in my development. To what degree it all plays in my issues as I work through them, it's hard to say. I place faith in the acknowledgement that something was missed—I think, from that end, that's all I can do. On the other side, however, is to equally acknowledge what I did have growing up, and what was available to me. I had a rich childhood on the South Side, not in terms of wealth or material possessions but with respect to opportunities and a firm, sound foundation of nurturing love and stern discipline from my mother.

No matter where I am in life, it all comes back to her. I wish I could give her everything; I think, so far, I've given her all that I can. Still, it doesn't always feel enough. Perhaps because more than a mother, she is a true friend to me, a teacher who dedicated herself to my development, to my seeing a wide world, and to my growth without limits. I said I wanted to be a star like a young Michael Jackson, and she said okay, then pointed at a stack of books for me to read and write reports on. She showed me the way.

Maybe it's because she's a teacher by profession, where she once educated and directed the lives of so many young people, that I wonder if her effect on them was similar, or as impactful, as it was on me, and if I had swapped places with one of those students—this kid gets to be her son while I am just her student from Monday to Friday—if he would be where I am today, and I would have an entirely different life. I only think about these things just because I'm beginning to understand how fragile life itself can be; it feels like the slightest change, one different decision, can alter everything; and the way life goes, you can never really be sure of how this one decision can make all the difference for you until much later on in the future, when things have already happened, and people come and go, and you're left with memories and a search for what it all means.

Sometimes I wonder if love and forgiveness are two sides of the same coin or are independent things but become so intertwined with each other, that they become inseparable. Either way you look at it, that would mean forgiveness itself is, like love, an action, a practice. Thinking about my parents again, and what I would've seen if they had stayed together, this act of forgiveness would've been one of the most important lessons. I know it now: It is not easy to forgive someone. And, like love, there's no one prescriptive method for forgiveness; like all things, we each have to find our own way. While this can make forgiveness, like love, all the more valuable to us, because the meaning is discovered by us in our own individual lives, that all can make forgiveness a messy, uncertain process.

It only gets easier with time, I suppose, and with repetition. To open your mind enough to be forgiving is the path to compassion, not just toward ourselves but toward other people, especially those who've wronged us in some way. The more you do not like someone, or feel any kind of warmth toward them, the more resistance we can feel when we recognize the need to be compassionate. Often, it feels like someone is not deserving of compassion or forgiveness; this is true sometimes. And in those moments, all we can do for ourselves, speaking of compassion, is just to be fair and true to our feelings, to accept that at this time, we can't forgive; we can't extend compassion.

But we want to; we feel that desire to be better versions of ourselves. Here, we have a chance to be forgiving of ourselves. That's the way to empathy; through the ways in which we treat ourselves, we can see a way to treat others. It takes courage to see we're standing on the same ground; it takes an open heart to recognize we're facing ourselves.

But for all this introspection, this soul-searching, life goes on and interrupts our internal dramas with the everyday rhythm, with the things that we need to address right now. My mother's health, for example. She's had thyroid issues for years, and over the years, I could see the growth and became increasingly concerned. My mother managed her own care and tried several natural paths to improve her health, which she did on many levels, but the thyroid issue persisted. She would mention the doctors' recommendations that she have surgery, but she was not ready to take that step. I'm sure it's human nature to put that off, but that doesn't make it easy to handle. All I could do, concerns aside, was trust that in time, before things became too serious, she would make the right decision. She did, at last, and thankfully connected with a surgeon who eased her fears and led her to schedule surgery. Medical science, at least in this country, might be more advanced now than ever before, but none of that eliminates the instant anxiety felt the second a loved one tells you they're having surgery.

I flew from Los Angeles to Chicago ahead of my mother's scheduled surgery. On the flight, I felt fine at first but as time went on, and as the airplane approached Chicago, I started to feel a little nervous. I began to softly pray, just to ask God to make sure she was at ease and remained comfortable, and to give the surgeon and nurses all the wisdom they needed to guide her through the procedure, and to care for my mother's husband, my stepfather, Ralph, who was probably fussing over her as they made their way to the hospital. I spoke to her earlier, before I took off at LAX, and then, just as the days and weeks before, my mother sounded peaceful and, I admit, unusually calm. Not that my mother is a high-strung person or someone prone to overt anxiety; generally, she always tries to strike and maintain an air of cool about her. But it was clear to me in our recent conversations that my mother had been working on herself spiritually: meaning, she sounded as if she spoke from a deeper connection with God and herself, arriving at a serene place that was new to me, and was a bit jarring.

At first, I wondered if she was making peace due to some

personal knowledge that maybe she wouldn't make it out of the surgery, and I suppose for anyone at her age, it would be wise to have a clear sight into life and death. But she didn't sound scared of death, and she didn't seem to me as though she was "letting go." My mother just—sounded *ready*. It was as if her will strengthened, as if a blacksmith tempered a steel rod. Whether she survived the surgery or not, she was present and wanted to remain present until the end, no matter what. So while I started feeling nervous as my flight descended into Chicago, I couldn't help but feel that tempered strength, too, or to at least draw some courage from it. As we landed, I felt myself becoming more present.

While my mother was prepped for the procedure, her surgeon spoke to us and tried to set expectations. The surgery itself was not unusual, but not without some risks for someone her age; instead of the typical two to four hours, the surgeon expected the whole procedure to take around five hours, given her extended situation. They were to begin promptly at 8 a.m., and we all made sure to arrive ahead of schedule to spend time with her. By 7:45, my mother was on the gurney, wearing a hospital gown and a little bonnet to cover her hair, as they prepared to wheel her into the operating room. Each of us had a moment to spend with her, and I took my time when it was my turn; I kissed her cheek and quickly studied her eyes as I said a prayer inside. Her eyes and her energy were strong and yet calm and present, so I felt assured that she would be fine. She said she was *ready*.

As I stepped back, Ralph stepped forward and told her he would be right here the whole time and would be right there when she woke up. I watched and listened to the two of them. They've been married for forty years; I grew up with them, but it occurred to me there, through an unusual feeling, that all that time before I didn't quite see them the way I saw them minutes before the surgery. I witnessed something new, and yet it was always there; I couldn't quite figure out what it was, and I couldn't explain to myself that unusual feeling. There was no time; the nurses pushed the gurney and wheeled my mother through the doors and down the corridor. What remained was the waiting; in your imagination, you can assume how this waiting will play out, and all the things you might do to keep yourself occupied. But it means nothing when in real time your mind wants to do nothing else but wonder about your mother. Five hours instantly became eternity, and it was only eight o'clock.

Firm in my faith in God and His watching over the surgeon as she worked, I felt confident that my mother would pull through just fine. Faith, in general, isn't a wishing away of the bad things that happen to us in life; when it is said to "Give it to God," there can be a misunderstanding as to what this means. Maybe it has a different meaning for other people, but for me it's not about handing off painful moments or suffering to God as if it's not mine to deal with; on the contrary, that I have to deal with it all means I am charged to do something with it, to find a lesson in it, or just to recognize a truth I would've otherwise passed over or neglected to see.

In the case of my mother's surgery, I understood the fragile nature of life; having already lost my father, I could feel how things can seem stable and sure in one moment, and how things can crumble away in the next moment. From that point of view, faith for me is a confirmation and an acknowledgement of life as it goes, and the importance in remaining entirely present within each moment. No matter how hard we try, we can't seem to grasp onto things and people as we all move through time.

We're always changing, and we're always carrying within ourselves a spirit that feels as fleeting as time itself, but is, in reality, the one place where we ground ourselves, and establish sure footing. I don't know where I would be without faith; I don't know what kind of man I would've become without God's grace. In moments where it feels like everything can slip away, literally within a heartbeat, faith is the anchor; and on our feet, being a person is often no more than going with the flow. Giving it to God is to go with the flow, all while being mindful, present, and ready for whatever comes. I don't know if anyone is ever really ready for a loved one to pass on. My father was ill for years, but I wasn't quite *ready* in the moment I received the call and learned of his passing. After that, like all things in life, I had to live within the new reality; there, too, faith kept me upright and strong for myself and my family.

So while I wasn't afraid that something would happen to my mother, and I knew God maintained His eye on her, I understood that things change swiftly. And as we began to wait through her surgery, it was important for me to work through all the thoughts and feelings within me, and try not to drift too far away, fighting with myself, so to speak, to remain in the present. There are so many distractions available to all of us now; sometimes it's easier or even therapeutic to check out and let our minds float away, to peek in on the news or to scroll through social media. I like to think there are reasons why we distract ourselves, reasons that aren't as negative as they might appear. Maybe it's in our human nature to look for the occasional distraction. If so, then the challenge for us is to always find the courage and strength to pull ourselves back into the moment. This is not so easy for us, at least for me anyway. But again, faith helps. And often, I return to my favorite scripture, 1 Corinthians 13 (NIV):

If I speak in the tongues of men or of angels, but do not have love, I am only a resounding gong or a clanging cymbal. If I have the gift of prophecy and can fathom all mysteries and all knowledge, and if I have a faith that can move mountains, but do not have love, I am nothing. If I give all I possess to the poor and give over my body to hardship that I may boast, but do not have love, I gain nothing.

Love is patient, love is kind. It does not envy, it does not boast, it is not proud. It does not dishonor others, it is not self-seeking, it is not easily angered, it keeps no record of wrongs. Love does not delight in evil but rejoices with the truth. It always protects, always trusts, always hopes, always perseveres.

Love never fails. But where there are prophecies, they will cease; where there are tongues, they will be stilled; where there is knowledge, it will pass away. For we know in part and we prophesy in part, but when completeness comes, what is in part disappears.

When I was a child, I talked like a child, I thought like a child, I reasoned like a child. When I became a man, I put the ways of childhood behind me. For now we see only a reflection as in a mirror; then we shall see face to face. Now I know in part; then I shall know fully, even as I am fully known. And now these three remain: faith, hope and love. But the greatest of these is love.

Ralph had no intentions on leaving the hospital, and said as much to us. He insisted that he would eat at the hospital a little later. Tamara and I had decided we'd go back to the hotel to eat and wait there. The surgery staff already had our phone numbers, and said they'd provide updates via text message to Ralph every few hours; he assured us he would keep us posted as he received messages. The hotel was close enough to the hospital in case an update of any kind, and from anyone, suggested we needed to come back. Still, it comforted me to know my stepfather wanted to stay behind and continue fussing over my mother, even from the waiting room.

A snowstorm, in typical Chicago fashion, was blowing through the city. I had a red-eye for New York scheduled, assuming all went well with my mother, and as we drove I worried a little bit about being snowed in; as much as I love home, and I take any opportunity available to come home, I felt a little anxious to get back to New York and to the studio to continue work on some new music. I had some unfinished tracks loaded on my phone so I could listen while writing and practicing lyrics, hoping to record them soon. When this creative energy flows through me, I feel this pull toward the studio, and an overall excitement to express, to work out whatever is in my heart, mind, and spirit. All three had been heavy, not just with concern for my mother but also for myself.

A week before my mother's surgery, Tamara and I were in Los Angeles, on our way to a photo shoot. There was nothing unusual about the day itself, and as for the photo shoot, I had known what to expect and felt nothing weird about the plan. On the outside, at least in my mind, I appeared as though nothing was wrong, but I wasn't entirely present. I decided to drive myself to the photo shoot, so I could return to the familiar place of my truck, where my lyrics flow most easily. Like so many of my songs, I create freely in my own space driving on an open road. As I maneuvered through the hills and up the freeway, I was driving, writing, rewriting, and deciding what I wanted to do next, if I should, or could, go through with what I considered doing. Not that I'm careless or thoughtless with things, but I prefer to just act, to be in a space where I can just do something without entertaining doubts. Faith, again, comes through and provides for me a path; trusting in God, in myself, I know what I should do from moment to moment. Sometimes I just need a moment to process and clear out the thoughts; sometimes, I need to be sure.

So, as we pulled up to the location for the shoot, I made my decision; I waved over Tamara, who rode in the car ahead of me and asked her to talk. She immediately came to my window, and asked if everything was okay. I did not get out of my truck. I said I wanted to play a song for her that I was working on right then. I started by playing a beat. We bobbed. It wasn't unusual for me to share beats and sample lyrics. I stopped that beat and searched the audio files on my phone and played another beat. I turned up the volume just a bit more. I said nothing as the beat played, and then I began to rap the first verse. I stopped and started over again as the beat continued; this time I went all the way from the first to the second verse, which wasn't actually complete yet, but it was close enough. I fell back and gave Tamara all the space to listen; the first person to hear these lyrics. I watched as Tamara listened, and moments later her eyes widened in surprise, or in shock.

In 2017, I worked on a film called *The Tale,* starring Laura Dern; the movie was written and directed by Jennifer Fox, whom Dern depicted, and it told the story of Fox's childhood abuse. As with all roles I decide to pursue and take on, this one had attracted my interest and I wanted to prepare for it as much as I could. And in that preparation, I had many conversations and script readings with Laura and Jennifer. It was clear to everyone that the movie would dive into heavy themes and would ask for each actor to bring their very best.

I wanted to do no less, and as I studied the script I contemplated the trauma and the weight abuse survivors carry, and how that trauma plays out in unexpected ways, particularly in adulthood, and how our minds, in protecting us, can create a kind of distance between our memories and ourselves, or what we believe about ourselves, the stories that take shape over time, almost like little movies in our heads and spirits. The more I dug into the role, the more I reflected on people I loved, on myself, and considered what pain can really do to us.

And one day, while talking through the script with Laura, old memories surprisingly flashed in my mind. I caught my breath and just kept looping the memories over and over, like rewinding an old VHS tape to take closer looks at the previous scene. I said to Laura, "I think I was abused." Right there, it all came back to my mind as if someone had suddenly inserted deleted scenes into that little movie in my head, scenes that I hadn't remembered or thought about before, scenes I couldn't even remember remembering. It seemed at first like I had been betrayed by my mind; I think we can all relate to that firm, confident feeling of *knowing* our lives, including the past, especially when it comes to our childhoods.

Maybe it's a matter of survival—even now, two years after that flash resurgence of memories, as I'm writing, I'm still working through all of this in myself and with my therapist, so I don't have answers or even a language ready-made for me to draw from; the best I can do now is just speak it all from the heart, as it comes. Anyway, it feels like a kind of survival. I don't know. All I can really say about my memories is for whatever the reason, maybe out of self-protection, they remained inaccessible from me for decades, and now that they're back, slowly I've tried to sift through them, like old photographs found in a shoebox underneath the bed, to make sense of what it all means for me, and for the people in my life who I love, who love me, who had no idea that this had happened.

It's why I recorded the song I shared with Tamara. At the time, when I first heard the track and started to write lyrics for it, I didn't have these memories directly on my mind; I didn't approach the song intending to mention what happened. But as I listened, I wrote freely, as I always do, and I trusted where my creative spirit took me—I don't know, maybe intentions, like memories, can be hidden, too, and suddenly appear whenever the situation is just right. And while I've said in other places in many times in my life how appreciative I am of music, and having such an outlet to express myself, it is an understatement to say now how invaluable and awesome the power of art has been for me and can be for every one of us. I didn't know how to speak on it directly, but I do know how to rap, and through rap express what must come through me. Speaking my truth, in other words.

Today I have a greater appreciation for the empowerment found in speaking one's truth.

I was about nine or ten years old; to be honest, I could've been a year younger—it's frustrating to still have some haziness around my memories, but I'm working to be easy with myself, and to trust that as I continue to recollect over time, the little details will be cleared up. That said, I remember I was excited for a road trip I was about to take with my family. My mother; my godmother, Barbara; her son and my godbrother, Skeet; and his relative, who I'll call Brandon, and me—we all rode together from Chicago to Cleveland, where we planned to stay at Skeet's aunt's house. Brandon was several years older than me, from Chicago as well, and was heavy into house music, which was a big scene on the South Side.

House seemed to push music and fashion forward in the city, and Brandon had this cool, fresh vibe as he was just getting started into DJing. I hung out with him and Skeet during the summer months, usually at Skeet's family's apartment not that far from where I grew up. And whenever we hung out, the three of us—Skeet, Brandon, and me—just chilled and listened to music. Sometimes, Skeet and Brandon started talking about girls they knew, and since I was younger than them, I just listened and, to be honest, didn't have anything to add to the subject. Brandon would tease me a little bit about this, and tried to get me to join in on the conversation.

I remembered one day when all of this happened again at Skeet's place—this was a few months before the car trip to Cleveland. Skeet had just left the room for some reason, maybe to get the door or to answer the phone; in any case, Brandon and I were alone, and he started talking about girls again. I was sitting down, and he was standing off to the side of me, just within my peripheral vision. All of a sudden, his hand was on my shoulder and back, not for long but—I remember how I felt. Something about the touch didn't sit right with me; I felt awkward and hoped for Skeet to come back, which he did in what seemed like the next moment. From there, the three of us proceeded as if nothing had happened; Brandon didn't say another word about the touch, and I most certainly didn't want to speak on it. I didn't even know what I would say. I had no words for how the touch made me feel, beyond this negative vibe that shocked through my body. And as far as I can remember right now, I didn't think again about that moment, and I don't recall other similar instances of what I can call now inappropriate, or at least uncomfortable touches. I felt no ill will toward Brandon; when I found out he was coming along with us to Cleveland, I was generally excited to have the opportunity to hang out with him and Skeet out of town.

But I do remember feeling nervous when, upon arriving at Skeet's aunt's house in Cleveland, and after the hugs and the welcomes, the usual happiness that comes from being around family, my aunt had worked out who would room with whom. Skeet and a couple of other kids were to sleep in one room, and Brandon and I were to share another room. I remember wanting at the time to ask for another arrangement. In that moment, it just felt like an instinct, an intuitive move, I guess. But I didn't say anything. What could I say? Thinking back now, there was nothing I could do. As much as I felt I could speak to my mother about anything, "anything" was conditional, I suppose and in retrospect, because again, I didn't have the words. Regardless, it would've been weird, for lack of a better word, for me to say anything that suggested an uneasiness around Brandon—no one would've suspected—and I just pushed the whole thing out of my head, hoping, perhaps, that nothing bad would happen.

Later that night, when it was time to sleep, Brandon and I shared the one bed in the room. I remember just turning over and closing my eyes tightly, waiting to fall asleep. I don't remember how much time passed, but at some point I felt Brandon's hand on me. I pushed him away; I don't remember saying a whole lot, besides "No, no, no." That aside, I just kept pushing away his hand, then his hands. And he kept saying something like, "It's okay, it's okay, everybody does this." Whether that was true or not didn't matter to me at all—I knew *I* didn't want any part of what he wanted. I felt his hand on my crotch; I said "No" more forcefully, but not loud enough for anyone else to hear us. He kept saying, "It's okay, it's okay" as he pulled down my shorts and molested me. After he stopped, he then kept asking me to perform it on him. I kept repeating "No," and pushing him away. Thinking back, I should've gotten up from the bed and ran out of the room; but I felt a deep and sudden shame for what happened, and for what he kept trying to make happen, as if I had brought it all on myself. I didn't want to say anything, to anyone, and hoped that he would just leave me alone, and go to sleep, which, eventually, he did once I fought back enough that he knew I was not going to touch him at all.

Nothing else happened. The rest of the trip went on as planned; everyone seemed happy, having a good time. I remember putting on the best face I could, but I was distant, perhaps as distant as another planet, feeling elsewhere within my own body, ashamed of myself and struck into silence. I said nothing to Brandon, to Skeet, to my godmother—to no one, most certainly not to my mother. I felt like I would never speak of it again, pushing it all out of my mind—or so I thought. More to the point, I buried it all in my mind, as deep as I could, hoping no one would see it or the shame that came along with it. And all of it stayed buried for decades. I haven't seen or spoken to Brandon in more than twenty-five years. I don't remember thinking about him, or wondering what became of him, no more than anyone else, I mean—it wasn't as if my mind kept egging me to remember all that I had buried.

Even now, with the memories back, I don't hold anything against Brandon. I wish it hadn't happened at all; and I don't know what it means to be victimized, to be a victim, but all I can say at this time is I don't *feel* like a victim, but maybe that'll change as I continue to reconcile myself with what happened, to open up fully to the trauma. In other words, I don't know why it happened to me, or why Brandon decided to do that to me. Still, I forgive Brandon for what happened. In speaking truth, there is also empowerment in deciding how I will carry all of this with me; I can decide how I think of him, of what occurred, and I can recognize the power of cycles. I want to be a person who helps break cycles of violence and trauma. I forgive him. This is love in action, and I intend to practice it.

. . .

It was approximately 3 p.m. when I could feel myself getting increasingly nervous about the surgery. I had received text updates from Ralph while Tamara and I were at the hotel, but I started to worry as the updates slowed down and we were past the five-hour mark; by this time we had finished lunch and I had worked out, just to keep busy. I tried to work on music, as Tamara worked on her laptop. Then I abruptly said, "Let's go back to the hospital now." We immediately gathered our things. In the bathroom, getting myself ready to head out, I took a moment to pray and calm myself down, to "feel" for my mother, as if I could reach out and connect to her spirit. I wanted to know that she was okay, that she was still here with us. Finally, Tamara and I made our way back to the hospital, where I knew I would be staying until the surgery was over. We met up with Ralph, who put on a brave face for us, but it was obvious to me he was getting more and more worried, too. He told us that he had been asking nurses and other staff if there was any more news; the best we could do was wait for the surgeon.

I was present, but felt jittery, stuck between anxiety and

worry, wanting to do something but felt strangely powerless
to do anything. It wasn't like I could barge into the operating
room and do the doctors' job for them! I felt like I could, like
I could do anything to make my mother well; but understanding that the waiting *was* what I could and should do, I tried
to claim that feeling of confidence, as though it were a touch
of grace and momentary calm from the Most High. Even so, it
was hard to hold on, to see through to faith.

As four o'clock rolled on, then five o'clock, the three of us
sat, quietly talking and waiting. We did learn that the surgery
actually began a little late, closer to 9 a.m., which was of some
comfort, but what should've been a four- or five-hour procedure
stretched toward eight hours, now without updates from the
operating room. An awkward silence was shared between us,
along with little looks and stares; our body language and our
facial expressions said everything, and it was as if each of us re-
fused to say a word, to somehow jinx things despite the anxiety.
And when we did receive an update, finally, informing us that
the surgery was complete, we waited another agonizing forty-
five minutes for someone to meet with us to give the full report.

At last, the surgeon came out and spoke to us. She explained the operation, including why she needed the extended
time, and assured us that my mother was well and would re-
cover from the procedure. She asked us to be patient while my
mother was leaving recovery and transferred to her hospital

room. Soon after, Tamara, Ralph, and I were waved over by a transporter who was taking my mother to her room. As we joined him in the hall, I immediately walked to my mother, expecting to be instantly relieved, but it wasn't what I expected. It was difficult to see her in such a vulnerable position, wrapped in blankets on a gurney, her eyes closed, her lips sealed, and still out of it from the anesthesia. I realized instantly that I had only known the formidable woman who raised me, and was always somehow, in some way, poised as a leader and in full control. We followed the transporter as he wheeled her to the room, and then waited until the nurses settled my mother and allowed us into the room. I walked in last, still a little stunned from the moment in the hall. Groggy from the anesthesia, my mother slowly regained consciousness as we gathered around her; there were clear plastic tubes that snaked from her nose and arms to intravenous fluids and oxygen to help her breathe, but beyond that, she appeared fine, if only extremely tired, stirring from a long, deep nap. Her eyes were still closed as she took a few silent moments for herself, to gather her bearings. My mother asked, "Where's Ralph?"

"I'm right here," Ralph said, with her purse in hand, guarding it like a soldier protecting a queen's crown jewels, as he moved toward the side of the bed.

"Okay, I hear him," my mother said very quietly. Her eyes were still closed.

It was a little funny, actually, watching Ralph shuffling around the room, fixing her bedsheets, crouching over and whispering to her, and listening to her in return. Just like the last few moments before she was wheeled into the operating room, I watched my mother being doted over by Ralph. I saw them differently.

Maybe this is all it's for; maybe it's this simple. For all the forgiving and the fighting, the mistakes and the lessons learned, for all the talking, and all of that "doing the work," this is where, if successful, we find ourselves: At our most vulnerable, our most raw, waking up to life and calling out for our partner in life, and having that person by our side, fretting over us as we're quietly thankful for one more moment in love. Forty years together, nearly all my life, and for as much as I missed not seeing my parents together, it was only there, in the hospital room, where I saw for myself a worthy goal, what makes music and movies, success and art, meaningful. I don't know if there's more to life than this, but this would be enough for me, if I were Ralph, if I were my mother.

. . .

I didn't know how I was going to tell her, and at this moment, I still don't. To rap about it, or to write about it, is by no means the same as having to talk to my mother about what happened to me as a child on that family vacation. I can imagine the conversation playing out in many different ways, and maybe the true, actual way is some blending or combination of these fantasies. In one sense, it doesn't really matter; my mother, if nothing else, would expect me to be open and direct with her. I like to think, however, that she'd understand why I didn't say anything that night, or the next day, or the day after, why, after so many years, I would speak on it now. And I hope she'd understand why I've decided to share my truth with the world, but maybe that's too big of a thought for what is a very personal and human need: to tell a parent that their child was harmed, and they couldn't do anything to stop it. It's a parent's worst nightmare. Being a parent myself, I'd want to know if my child is okay.

But I have to admit to some confusion. When I tell her about what happened, who exactly is talking: the ten-year-old boy or the forty-seven-year-old man he became; is it the child and son, or the man and father? Should she comfort me, or is it more important that I reassure and comfort her? Granted, I turn to faith and give it to God once more, standing firm on the spiritual plane and feeling grounded by this belief, this acknowledgement of His presence. But no one, not even God, said that life would be easy, or without suffering. For all the praying I can do, and the faith I can reaffirm—for as much as I can give it to God—love always returns to a human affair, a couple of people face-to-face in the middle of miracles and disasters, trying to make sense of it all. I don't know if that's God's job to do; it seems not. And if not, then faith, as powerful as it is, ferries us across troubled waters deep enough to bury a boy's memories of a night in Cleveland. I don't know how to tell her. But I will, and I know love will see us through. I believe it.

The miracle is a shift in our own thinking: the willingness to keep our own heart open, regardless of what's going on outside us.

—Marianne Williamson

———

L ast night, Omoye called me. And once again, it was a late-night (or early morning) call; it was around 2 a.m. her time in Washington, DC. Some time has passed since that other phone conversation, and we'd since had the opportunity to speak and to see each other, to continue communicating in what I hope is a healthier, more productive way. For my part, I've become less defensive, and not so quick to snap back with rebuttals when all she's trying to do is share her perspective with me.

All I want is to be a good father to her; it wouldn't be much for me to give up anything, everything, if in the end I can give her all the love I have. It's not that I want her to acknowledge me as a good father; I just want to protect her from the cold, and to shield her from the heat, no matter that's she a young adult taking care of herself. So what does it mean to be a good father? I don't know; it's not an exact idea in my mind anymore. It's best, I've discovered, to approach it with the right intentions; if I do this with presence of mind, I have a chance to be good to her. As parents, we can't ask of ourselves any more than that; it's an exercise in kindness to ourselves.

Anyway, she called me—sober, this time—and said to me, "I was just listening to some of your stuff." That "stuff" was the latest album I had released, *August Greene* with Karriem Riggins and Robert Glasper. She said, "I was listening to *August Greene* . . . and Dad, you're not a bad dad. I didn't say that you were a bad dad."

She had heard the lyrics to the last song on the album. I said, "Daughter talks, divine order caught, me by the collar, what it is to be a father, made some mistakes, some things I was good at, you take away the bad and you gotta take the good back."

I remember when working on the album, writing lyrics for that last track, everything that Omoye and I had talked about was swirling in my head. It felt like a burden that I wanted to release, just so I could breathe; music has always provided that outlet for me, a space to work out my emotions and to clarify, perhaps to myself, how I see a situation in the moment. I wanted to make things right between us, and I didn't quite know how at the time—but I had art, my music, which is always there for me, guiding me back to myself.

After she heard the song, she picked up the phone and called me. And there she was last night, tearing up three thousand miles away. She said, "You're not a bad dad. I didn't mean to say it like you were a bad dad to me."

I said, "I'm not perfect. My imperfections, you know, some of the things you received from me, maybe they weren't the best from a dad, but some of it was. In either case, I understand my imperfections, and the mistakes I've made, and . . . I feel like I want to do better. I always want to do better for you."

She said, "I don't want you to think you were a bad dad, that's all. Because I shouldn't have any other dad but you. You're the dad I'm supposed to have." Those were her words to me: "You're the dad I'm supposed to have." It may not be everything, but it's enough—it's love. It's all good, and it was a full circle, having her say those words to me. For now, love had the last word, and the journey continues . . .

We love because it's the only true adventure.

—Nikki Giovanni

EPILOGUE

66 Great art can only be
created out of love. 99

– *James Baldwin*

This is a playlist of music that has been the background of my life throughout this process of writing, exploring, and growing.

A LOVE SUPREME, PT. 1: ACKNOWLEDGEMENT	■	JOHN COLTRANE
THE MAKINGS OF YOU	■	CURTIS MAYFIELD
GOD IS LOVE	■	MARVIN GAYE
ASKIM	■	KAMASI WASHINGTON
ZOOM	■	THE COMMODORES
CRANES IN THE SKY	■	SOLANGE
CHANGED	■	WALTER HAWKINS
SWEETEST THING	■	FUGEES
BE ALRIGHT	■	ZAPP
WAIT ON ME	■	SAMORA PINDERHUGHES AND COMMON
SEEMS SO LONG	■	STEVIE WONDER
REALLY LOVE	■	D'ANGELO AND THE VANGUARD
SOUND & COLOR	■	ALABAMA SHAKES
WILD IS THE WIND	■	NINA SIMONE

AHT UH MI HED	■ SHUGGIE OTIS
THE WAY YOUNG LOVERS DO	■ VAN MORRISON
UMI SAYS	■ MOS DEF
YAH.	■ KENDRICK LAMAR
BREAK EVERY CHAIN	■ TASHA COBBS LEONARD
OPEN YOUR EYES	■ BOBBY CALDWELL
GLORY TO THE LAMB	■ GEOFFREY GOLDEN

COMMON'S HOPE AND REDEMPTION TOUR 2017 AND 2018,
WITH IMAGINE JUSTICE, ANTI-RECIDIVISM COALITION (ARC),
AND THE CALIFORNIA ENDOWMENT

© Sade Joseph

© Sade Joseph

© Sade Joseph

© Sade Joseph

© Sade Joseph

© Sade Joseph

© Sade Joseph

© Sade Joseph

© Sade Joseph

© Sade Joseph

© Sade Joseph

© JT McGlockton

© Sade Joseph

© JT McGlockton

© JT McGlockton

© Sade Joseph

© Sade Joseph

© Sade Joseph

© Sade Joseph

© Sade Joseph

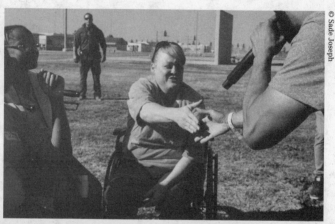

© Sade Joseph

© Sade Joseph

inset photos © Sade Joseph

© JT McGlockton

© JT McGlockton

© Sade Joseph

ACKNOWLEDGEMENTS

Thank you, GOD, for you are The Greatest. Thank you for your son, Jesus. There is no love greater than yours. Special thank-you to Mensah Demary, Tamara Brown, and Kirby Kim. This book would not be without the efforts of you three. Beautiful work. To my Simon & Schuster/Atria Books team, thank you for your support and for seeing this project through. To my band, Think Common, Freedom Road, Common Ground Foundation, and Imagine Justice family, I'm blessed to have your love, commitment, and talents in my life. To Alex Crotin, Amanda Nesbitt, Micaela Erlanger, Brian Bowen Smith, thank you all for your contributions to this project. Ma and Ralph, I love y'all. Thanks for all the love you give. Omoye . . . Bless you, my daughter. I'm proud of you, and I love you very much.

© JT McGlockton

ABOUT THE AUTHOR

COMMON is an Oscar, Golden Globe, Emmy, and Grammy Award–winning music artist. He is an actor and producer and has appeared in numerous critically acclaimed films as well as hit TV series. Common is the author of *One Day It'll All Make Sense*, which was a *New York Times* bestseller. He was raised in Chicago and currently resides in Los Angeles and Brooklyn.

LOVE